D1790292

kids POWer hour

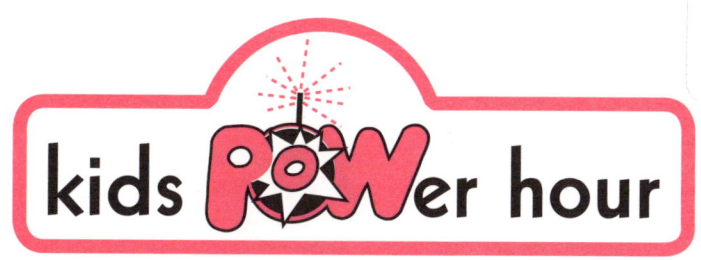

Creative Children's Church Curriculum
POWer of Worship
POWer of the Word

J-O-Yful Hands

J — Jesus First
O — Others Second
Y — You Last

WORD AFLAME PUBLICATIONS
Pentecostal Publishing House
8855 Dunn Road • Hazelwood, MO 63042-2299
Printed in U. S. A.

Word Aflame Staff

Editor . . . . .R. M. Davis
Associate Editor . . . . .P. D. Buford
Children's Editor . . . . .Barbara Westberg

Editor in Chief—UPCI . . . .J. L. Hall

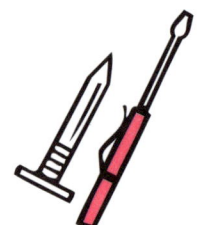

 Writers

Beverly Burk
Pamela J. Taylor
Paula Townsley
Barbara Westberg

 Lay Out

Joni Owens

 Art

Georgia Smelser
Elizabeth Swisher

 Photography

Wayne Collins

 On Cover

Misti Dawn Palmer
Joseph Muldrow

CURRICULUM COMMITTEE
James E. Boatman,
P. D. Buford,
R. M. Davis,
J. L. Hall,
G. W. Hassebrock,
Garth E. Hatheway,
E. E. Jolley,
E. J. McClintock,
Chester L. Mitchell,
W. C. Parkey,
David L. Reynolds,
Charles A. Rutter,
Berl Stevenson,
R. L. Wyser.

© 1996 by
Pentecostal Publishing House,
Hazelwood, MO 63042
All rights reserved
ISBN 1-56722-193-9

Permission to copy scripts and art granted for local church use only.

Table of Contents

Editorial by Barbara Westberg 4
Theme Development 5
    The Workshop 5
    J-O-Yful Hands Banner 5
    Hands On 5
    Handy Dan 6
    Handy Helpers 6
    Hands-Full Jars 7
    From Our Hands to Yours 8
    Shop Talk 8
An Overview of *kids POWer hour* 9
Puppet Spectacular by Teresa Bohannon .10
POWer hours 12-92
J-O-Yful Hands (photo helps), La Marque, Texas 78
Song Transparency Masters 93-95, 127
Memory Passage Transparency Masters 95-96
POWer houses 97-122
Art 123-127
Puppet Stage Pattern 128

UNIT ONE   J = Jesus First   Basic Truths
1. Hand in Hand with Jesus 12
2. Heart in Hand 19
3. Open Hands 25
4. Near at Hand 31

UNIT TWO   O = Others Second   Relationships 37
5. Jesus' Right Hands 38
6. Hands Reaching Out 43
7. Healing Hands 49
8. Helping Hands 54
9. Holding Up the Pastor's Hands 59

UNIT THREE   Y = You Last   Character Development 63
10. In God's Hands 64
11. A Sore Thumb 71
12. Idle Hands 79
13. Uplifted Hands 85

Editorial

And the World Wept

Less than one hundred miles southwest of where I sat at my desk working on *kids POWer hour*, a bomb exploded in a federal building. One hundred sixty-nine innocent people, including many children, died and the world wept.

A little over one hundred miles to the southeast, two-year-old Ryan Luke in a body cast from previous abuses was given by a judge into his grandfather's custody. A few days later little Ryan was dead, the victim of child abuse. A community and a state wept.

In a Partners-in-Missions newsletter a foreign missionary in Africa told of civil war and said, "The children suffer the most." And the church wept . . . or did we?

Jesus told the women who lined Calvary's road, *"Daughters of Jerusalem, weep not for me, but weep for yourselves, and for your children."* Looking down the road of time, He saw the day, less than thirty years ahead, when the Roman army would sweep into Jerusalem. And He said, "Weep for your children."

As He looks at the children in *kids POWer hour*, does He say to us, "Weep for your children"? I think so.

Rachel cried out to Jacob, "Give me children or I die." The heart's cry of the church is the same. The hope for children is the church. The hope for the church is children.

Strange, the editorial for *J-O-Yful Hands* is about weeping. What is the connection between weeping and joy?

"They that sow in tears shall reap in joy" (Psalm 126:5).

"He that goeth forth and weepeth, bearing precious seed, shall doubtless come again with rejoicing, bringing his sheaves with him" (Psalm 126:6).

Joyful hands, filled with sheaves, must be preceded by weeping hearts. May God bless you as you sow in tears.

Barbara Westberg

Review Notebook

Keep a notebook at your fingertips. Use it to:
- Write review questions over each hour's material. You will need these for games.
- List the children's names, addresses, phone numbers, birthdays.
- Make notes of special events in the lives of the children. Watch the newspaper for the names of children on the honor roll, participants in special events, births or deaths in families, etc.
- Jot down ideas for decorations, games, activities, etc.

The Workshop

Welcome to Handy Dan's Workshop.

At the front of the room build a work bench puppet stage. Cut the shape of a bench from a large cardboard box, such as an appliance box. Cut legs from the front, but leave the back uncut to cover puppeteers. Add wood grain with a marker. Place a variety of tools on the bench. Scatter among them tracts and a Bible.

Make the backdrop (top cabinet) of cardboard. Paint cabinet doors and hinges. With an Exacto knife score the doors so they open for the puppets.

Set a plain, worn bar stool beside it. Handy Dan sits here during *kids POWer hour*.

Hang a sign over the work bench.

J-O-Yful Hands Banner

Supplies:
- ❏ 6'- 8' strip of foamcore or posterboard (taped together)
- ❏ contrasting color paper
- ❏ small blocks of styrofoam
- ❏ glue
- ❏ fishing line

Cut out J-O-Y from contrasting colors. Attach small blocks of styrofoam on the back and glue to the banner. This will produce a 3-D effect.

Finish painting "ful Hands" on the banner.

During the first session, trace the children's hands (or let them do it) around the caption, using brightly colored markers. If time permits, set out pie pans of tempera paint. Allow the children to put their hand print on the banner. Provide water and paper towels for cleanup.

Hang the banner from the ceiling, using fishing line.

Hands On

Is there a wall in your room which could be painted and decorated with the hand prints of the children (in a variety of bright colors)? Painting one wall is usually not that big a job, and how the children will love putting their hand prints on it! After this series, it will simply be a matter of repainting that wall. If you think about it, this will not be as much work or expense as most decor ideas.

If painting a wall is out of the question, bring in a large piece of cardboard, foamcore, or sheetrock. Paint and attach to the wall or tack across a corner and decorate with hand prints. As new children come, allow them to add their hand print.

The idea is to let the kids put their "hands on" the room.

Handy Dan

Handy Dan is Mr. Fix-it. He wears work clothes, a hard hat, a nail apron (or tool belt) with a hammer in its loop, has a carpenter's pencil stuck behind his ear, and carries a loaded toolbox with a Bible sticking out of it.

He often interacts with the director to clarify scriptures or concepts. Most *POWer hours* he teaches an object lesson from his toolbox. He is a fun, but comforting guy.

Spiritually speaking, the only tool Mr. Dan needs is the Word of God! A large Bible sticks out of his toolbox.

He talks to the children one-to-one about broken hearts, homes, and lives. As they arrive, he circulates, asking what is broken in their lives or the lives of someone they know. They do not have to name the person. Handy Dan should be a spiritually sensitive guy, able to minister to the children. He encourages them in the Lord and gives them a "prescription," a Bible verse applicable to their need.

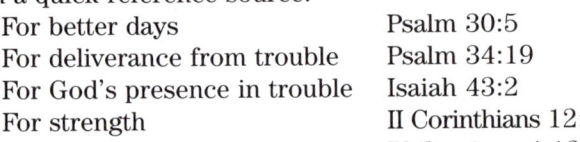

A copy of these promises written on index cards are stuck in his Bible to give him a quick reference source:

For better days	Psalm 30:5
For deliverance from trouble	Psalm 34:19
For God's presence in trouble	Isaiah 43:2
For strength	II Corinthians 12:9
	Philippians 4:13
For healing	James 5:14-15
For forgiveness	I John 1:9
For salvation	Acts 2:38-39
For direction	James 1:5
For answered prayer	Mark 11:24
For needs to be supplied	Philippians 4:19
God's divine providence	Romans 8:28

If planning for this series starts early enough, Handy Dan advertises the Hands-Full program the *POWer hour* before JOYful Hands begins.

Handy Helpers

Handy Dan's helpers are called the "handymen" and "handmaidens."

To save problems, write a job description for your helpers. This assures that they know their duties and eliminates excuses for jobs not done. Helpers are in children's church to assist the director, to model appropriate behavior, and to create an atmosphere of worship so children can receive the Holy Ghost. They should sit among the children and not congregate in the back to visit. If a helper has to be absent, he should notify the director as soon as possible so his place can be filled.

Handy Helpers wear padded bright-colored gloves or mittens. Anyone who can operate a sewing machine can make these. Or colorful oven mitts may be purchased. These are called the "joyful gloves."

Each glove contains at least one small prize, *e.g.*, a piece of candy, stick of gum, dime, balloon, sticker. (If there are only one or two helpers, their gloves should contain several prizes.) The Handy Helpers meet the children at the door and shake hands with them. Each handyman or handmaiden gives the prize hidden in their glove to someone before the hour ends. They may choose to give it to a visitor, a child who looks unhappy, a child who has been sick, a child who is singing joyfully. There should not be any particular reasoning to this so the children never know who is going to be given a joyful handshake.

An extra glove or mitten (the larger and brighter, the better), called the "kid's glove," and containing a special prize, is used as a good behavior motivator. In some sessions suggestions are given for determining who wears the "kid's glove." For other sessions choose a child who is caught being especially helpful or joyful.

Hands-Full Jars

Supplies:
- jar labeled "Brought a Bible"
- jar labeled "Recited Memory Passage"
- jar labeled "Brought a Guest"
- jar labeled "Guest"
- jar labeled "Grand Prize Drawing"
- small-mouthed jar containing candy (or miscellaneous treats)
- small-mouthed jar containing coins, mostly pennies
- colorful cutouts of child's hand
- markers
- Zip-loc™ bags

Dan, the Handy Man "advertises" this special activity a week in advance. If this has not been done before *POWer hour* 1, he can do his "commercial" at the end of the first hour and begin the project with *POWer hour* 2. Have the jars ready so he can show as he tells. He should create an exciting commercial to "sell" the children on the program.

As the children arrive each week, those who comply with whatever is written on the jar label, write their name on a hand-shaped cutout and put it in a jar. Handy Dan and the helpers assist the children. Those who can recite the memory passage as they enter, put their name in the "Recited Memory Passage" jar. This encourages the children to remember the verse from *POWer hour* to *POWer hour*. Smaller children could be given an abbreviated portion to memorize.

For each visitor a child brings, he puts one hand-shaped paper with his name on it in the "Brought a Guest" jar. This ups his chances to win.

Each visitor writes his name on a hand-shaped piece of paper and puts it in the "Guest" jar.

At the end of each *POWer hour*, one name is drawn from each jar. The winners reach into a small-mouthed jar (to make it more difficult and less expensive) for a "hand-full" of candy (or some treat). Everyone gives the winners "a hand."

Encourage participation by reminding children that they might be the winner next *kids POWer hour*. Guests will be encouraged to come back, too! Let them know that they can have more chances to win if they bring lots of guests. Guests can bring guests and Bibles and memorize verses, too!

Put the weekly winners' hand-shaped names in the "Grand Prize Drawing" jar. All other names are left in the jars and build up until the end of each unit. From time to time other jars are added, allowing the children who have been involved in a special project additional opportunities to win.

At the end of the last *POWer hour* in each unit, have a grand prize drawing. Allow the winner to reach into a jar of coins! Empty the Hands-full Jars and start fresh at the beginning of each unit.

Zip-loc™ bags help the winners get their hands-full home and keep the church clean.

From Our Hands to Yours

Check with your pastor for an offering project. If you have a foreign missions project, you might be interested in a display of tracts in foreign languages. Write to Foreign Missions Department, World Evangelism Center, 8855 Dunn Road, Hazelwood, MO 63042 and ask for a packet of sample foreign language tracts.

Set up a table that has tracts, Bibles, and/or Bible studies printed in another language. Explain to the students that printing these takes a lot of time and costs a lot of money! It is worth it, though, because it gets God's Word into the hands of people in other countries. If it had not been for John Wycliff who translated the Bible into English, we would not have God's Word in our hands!

Or your pastor may know of a home missions church which your *kids POWer hour* offerings could help. In this case, set up a display table featuring a picture of the home missions pastor and his family, along with the offering graph.

Kids need to visualize their progress! Set a goal and draw a line between $10.00 and your goal. Use the child-size hand cutouts to place along the line to mark progress. Each hand could represent $5.00 toward the goal.

Thirteen weeks (or *POWer hours*) is a long time to continue an offering project or contest. To keep it from becoming monotonous, divide into teams or age groups. Assign a different color hand to each group. Tally the offering according to teams. At the end of each unit, award the top givers a treat or special recognition.

When you send the offering to the recipient, include pictures of your *kids POWer hour* children.

Shop Talk

A staff meeting is necessary before beginning this series. Announce an informal planning and work session. Serve refreshments.

Read the feature pages and scan the first unit. Highlight the ideas which are workable in your *kids POWer hour* setting.

Have on hand all the supplies needed to decorate and prepare for the first unit.

- ✓ Find a Handy Dan. He should be an extroverted, spiritual man (young or old) with a sense of humor and a love for kids. He needs to be present at the planning session as he will be an important part of this series. If a man is not available for this part, a puppet can be used. However, this will require tailoring the material.

- ✓ Hand pick your staff. The handymen and handmaidens should be dependable, enthusiastic, and dedicated. Older teens make wonderful *kids POWer hour* helpers. Of course, everyone used must be approved by the pastor and/or Christian Education director. A music director helps, but if you do not have one, the *kids POWer hour* tape is your life-saver.

- ✓ Go over the plans for this series with the staff. Be sure helpers understand the rules and how each program or activity works.

- ✓ Assign jobs: *e.g.*, paint the wall or giant bulletin board, label jars and cut out hands, make the offering graph, make transparencies or flipcharts for new songs, design the banner, create stand-ups using the art in the back of the manual.

An Overview of *kids POWer hour*

kids POWer hour is made up of two general parts: POWer of Worship and POWer of the Word. Watch for these icons.

J-O-Yful Hand—This icon indicates time to give a joyful handshake.

Hands-Full Jar—time to put names in or draw names out of the Hands-full Jar.

The *Power Line* is the focus statement of the lesson. You will find it everywhere that message is repeated.

Praise Generators—songs, Dynamo specials, suggestions for prayer time, and testimony service ideas.

Truth Conductors—object lessons, science demonstrations, illustrations, skits which transmit an important truth.

Energy Outlets—games, activities, projects which allow the children to move around and work off energy.

Plug Ins—teaching tips to plug the teacher into the lesson text, students' characteristics, what to expect, etc.

Spirit Generators—worship choruses designed to prepare the hearts of the children for the Word of God.

Life Transformers—the Illustrated Sermon which transforms children into spiritual dynamos.

Puppet Time—skits, announcements, songs which are written for (or can be adapted to) puppets.

kids POWer hour **tape**—suggested songs, scripts, sound effects, and other resources called for in the text can be found on the tape. Order from **Pentecostal Publishing House, 8855 Dunn Road, Hazelwood, MO 63042-2299, 314-837-7300.**

Special Helps

On pages 93-96 are transparency masters to help you teach the songs and memory passages. If you have an overhead projector, copy these pages using copier transparency sheets. Add color with transparency markers.

If you do not have an overhead, copy these pages, one per child. Send the memory passages home with the children to color and use as a memory aid. The songs can be copied for song sheets. Make construction paper covers to create mini-songbooks, which the children can take home at the end of the series.

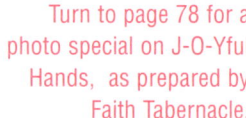

Turn to page 78 for a photo special on J-O-Yful Hands, as prepared by Faith Tabernacle.

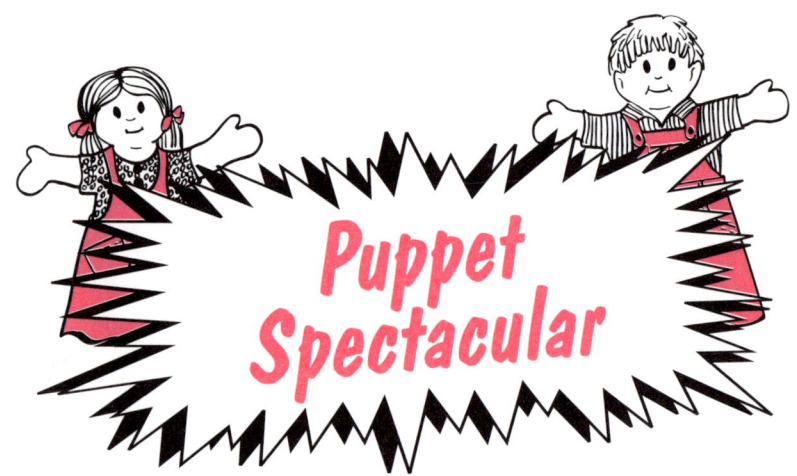

Puppet Spectacular

by Teresa Bohannon
Faith Tabernacle
La Marque, Texas

Puppets! The very word invokes smiles, mental pictures of funny looking characters and anticipation of a fun time. The appeal of puppetry knows no age limit, folks from one to one hundred-and-one love them. The therapeutic value of puppets is proven by their use in hospitals, rest homes, and therapy clinics. Do not overlook the teaching and entertaining value of puppets. A child who seems unreachable may respond to a puppet (a direct result of a dedicated, praying puppeteer). If your Sunday school or *kids POWer hour* needs a boost, consider puppets. You need not be an expert puppeteer, nor do you have to invest a lot of money to take advantage of this wonderful tool.

It is not known when the first puppets were made. Archaeologists have found puppets in ancient Greek tombs which date back to the sixth century B.C. Evidence in Europe and Asia show there have been puppets since the beginning of civilization. Puppets are woven through the history of the Orient and Egypt. Early Italian plays were presented to amuse and educate. Many of the people could not read, so puppets taught Scripture, religious principles, and more. The effectiveness of puppets remains through time. In fact, with new and different materials to create puppets, the appeal is greater now than at any other time.

So, where do you begin? When we started the puppet ministry at Faith Tabernacle, we had no puppets, a small budget, and a couple of women excited about puppetry. We ordered a puppet pattern, scheduled a puppet-making night, spent fifteen to twenty dollars for supplies, and plunged in. Each lady that came was assigned a job. Some cut fabric; some cut foam; others glued foam, while still others sewed the puppets together. Each of the eight ladies present was involved. We made six puppets and had supplies left.

In addition, we found two bird puppets on clearance for less than five dollars each at a toy store. The fun shop had a duck with long arms and legs that can be wrapped around your neck for less than ten dollars. My parents, who used puppets in Sunday school twenty-five years ago, donated a box of second-hand puppets. These were quite different from puppets used today. Some were very small and did not have mouths that opened. Others were exactly what we needed, including a large fish and a turtle. The Lord always blesses us when we work for Him. We went from no puppets to a closet full!

There are many kinds of puppets, ranging from small finger puppets, felt hand puppets, sock puppets, to large foam and velour puppets. Patterns for the foam and velour puppets may be ordered from the Pentecostal Publishing House, 8855 Dunn Road, Hazelwood, MO 63042 (Phone 314-837-7300). These are fairly easy to make. I recommend starting with at least two "people puppets" (a boy and a girl) and one animal puppet. Children love animal puppets. We have also made black light puppets, using one-inch foam spray painted with neon-colored paint. These require no sewing and very little time.

If you have trouble getting your supplies together, check resale shops and garage sales. Ask upholstery shops for scraps of foam. Used velour bathrobes can be recycled for fabric. Use wigs for hair, and toddler clothes for costumes. Your imagination is the only limit. We have a blue puppet, a teal puppet, and one with curly hot pink hair. We prefer to make our puppets with detachable wigs. By doing this, we use the base puppet for many different characters. You will probably want a variety of puppets for different purposes. The least expensive way is to make your own.

There are several advantages to making your own puppets, besides the money saved. You can make original puppets unlike anyone else's, and create special puppets for specific skits.

Puppet stages may be made from cardboard boxes, plywood, or the most popular, PVC pipe and fabric. We have two of the latter, one large and one small. Instructions for a PVC puppet stage are provided on page 128.

Proper care of puppets is essential. They are not toys. They are tools and should be treated as such. Children should not touch them, and no one should touch their faces. Many puppet teams Scotchguard their puppets to protect them.

Have a designated place to store puppets, and insist that they be returned to that area immediately following a practice or show. Make one person responsible for the care of the puppets. We store our puppets in a closet that has puppet rails attached to the walls. Each puppet has its own spot on the rail. We use an old accordion case to transport puppets for outreach. The size is perfect and the lining helps protect the puppets.

The next step in beginning your puppet ministry is training puppeteers. Hopefully, you will have a lot of volunteers and if so, use them. But it only takes two to make a team, so do not be discouraged if you only have two. Even if you are a one-person show, do not despair. Be faithful. Do the best you can. The Lord will multiply your efforts and bless you with puppeteers. Teens make an awesome puppet team. Use them, encourage them, and at the same time, warn them that puppet ministry is work.

To begin, order training tapes and practice together. If you do not have training tapes, choose simple songs or skits and practice again and again. Take the curtain off the puppet stage and practice. If you have too many puppeteers to do this, have them kneel on the floor during practice. Here are some guidelines for practice sessions:

1. **Position of hand in puppet.** Fingers always go on top, thumbs below. Drop your thumb. Do not move your fingers.
2. **Entrances and Exits.** There are no elevators or sudden appearances by puppets. Practice going upstairs with three or four steps, getting closer to the front of the stage and higher with each step. To exit, turn completely around and do a backwards entrance. It is acceptable to fall if you have appropriate sound effects, and it is part of the script.
3. **Puppeteers' Position.** Correct body position is a must. Puppeteers should be on their knees with their arms straight up. Short puppeteers can kneel on a piece of foam or a stool. Very short folk may stand. The puppeteer's body should be in a straight line—no chairs, bent arms, arm crutches or props, distorted body angles, knees or feet spread apart.
4. **Puppets' Position.** Puppets should be at waist length on stage. Keep the puppet 4"-5" from the front of the stage, and avoid leaning on the stage. One puppeteer who failed to follow this advice suddenly found the front of the stage on the ground with the audience staring at him. Do not allow the puppets to slip down; keep them at the proper level.
5. **Lip Synchronization.** Start with the puppet's mouth closed. Open the mouth once for each syllable; try not to chop up the words. If you are using a tape, practice speaking aloud with the tape. This will help you remember to open the mouth of the puppet every time you open your mouth. Please do not let the mouth hang open between words, as it makes the puppet seem unrealistic. Pay special attention to differences in voice tone and open the mouth appropriately—wide open for yells, barely open for whispers.
6. **Eye Contact.** Maintain eye contact between the puppet and the audience. You may have to tilt the puppet's head down slightly to do this. When your puppet is not speaking, do not look around. This is a sure way to lose the attention of the audience. Watch the puppet who is speaking.
7. **Be Realistic.** This is the main goal of puppetry. Do not be stiff and unmoving, but lifelike. Puppets can scratch their heads, blow kisses, yawn, wave, point, and much more.
8. **Rod arms.** Use rod arms to move the puppet arms. They may be ordered from puppet companies or made. To make a rod arm, use a wooden dowel with a cup hook screwed in the end. Place a rubber band around the wrist of the puppet and slip the cup hook through the rubber band. Hold the rod in your free hand and move it appropriately.
9. **Work from tapes and appoint a sound person.** We prefer to use puppet sound tracks or other music tapes. Tape each song on a separate tape to eliminate hunting for individual songs on a tape. If you use compact discs, you will not have this problem. If you are writing your own skits, tape them and work from the tape. Live performances lose their effectiveness when someone loses his place and stumbles around trying to get back on course. It is easier to work the puppet and listen to the tape than to work the puppet and read a script.

A word of caution: preview the sound tracks before you buy if possible. Some of these songs have beats that are not appropriate, and others are simply worldly songs with a few words changed to make them "Christian." Get the approval of your pastor or Christian education director before you use any.

Do not try to perform too soon, and never, never do it cold turkey. Practice, practice, practice and you will be effective. A weekly practice is necessary if you have a weekly performance. Prayer and fasting should be an integral part of your puppet ministry.

(continued on page 24)

J = Jesus First
O = Others Second
Y = You Last

Unit One
Basic Truths

Unit Aim: To give children basics for developing a relationship with Jesus Christ.

Memory Passage: Mark 12:29-30

Hand in Hand With Jesus

Scripture Text: Mark 10:17-30; John 6:67-68; Amos 3:3

 Walking hand in hand with Jesus pays more than it costs.

Schedule

Date: _____

I. POWer of Worship (30-35 minutes)
  A. Welcome (6 minutes)
    • Joyful Handshakes
    • Hands-Full Jar
    • Announcements
  B. Sing unto the Lord (6 minutes)
    • Praise Choruses
    • Dynamo Specials
  C. Lift Up Holy Hands (4 minutes)
    • Psalm 28:2
  D. Hand-n-Hand Art (10 minutes)
    • Demonstration of Teamwork
  E. Speak Up for Jesus (4 minutes)
  F. From Our Hands to Yours (3 minutes)
  G. A Lesson from the Toolbox (3 minutes)
    • A Glove Demonstration
II. POWer of the Word (20-25 minutes)
  A. From Hand to Heart (5 minutes)
    • Energy Outlet
  B. Worship Chorus (2 minutes)
  C. Illustrated Sermon (8 minutes)
    • The Rich Young Ruler and Peter
  D. Room for Jesus (5 minutes)
  E. Invitation and Prayer (5-? minutes)
  F. Energy Outlet
    • The Needle's Eye

Shop Talk

✓ Have a planning session as described in the feature pages.
✓ Check with Handy Dan to be sure he is ready. He needs a work glove in his toolbox.
✓ The "Hands-Full Jars" should be labeled and a large supply of child-sized hands cut out.
✓ Each handyman and handmaiden needs a joyful glove. (See page 6.) Put a prize in the kid's glove and have it handy to give as a reward for good behavior.
✓ Make four large fluorescent flashcards, "heart," "soul," "mind," "strength." For preschoolers, include symbols: heart, brain, muscle, and gingerbread shape to represent the soul. Tape one card to each wall.
✓ Make Play Clay (see the recipe on page 14), or purchase molding clay or Play Doh.
✓ Set up worktables and cover with newspaper. If possible, let everyone participate in the "Hand-n-Hand Art." For a large group, choose three or four teams. Provide pans of water and paper towels for clean-up.
✓ Gather a small basket, a number of things which are important to children, (*e.g.,* toys, books, candy), and a box with a lid on it labeled, "Jesus."
✓ Give the music director the *kids POWer hour* tape so he can be prepared to teach the theme songs. Print the theme songs, "My J-O-Yful Hands," "J-O-Y-F-U-L H-A-N-D-S," and the chorus of the old hymn, "Hand in Hand with Jesus" (see page 364 of *Sing Unto The Lord*) on large posterboard hands. Transparency masters are on pages 93-94.
✓ Write the *POWer line* on a board or poster, omitting the vowels.
✓ Make copies of the *POWer house* papers and the script of the Illustrated Sermon.

✓ The Bible story told by two puppets, **The Rich Young Ruler and Peter**, is on the *kids POWer hour* tape. Make Bible characters of any puppets by making robes, as shown, and pinning a length of cloth around their heads to form a turban. Peter's robe should be made of rough drab cloth. The rich young ruler's robe should be a brilliant color with gold trim. Tape a copy of the script inside the puppet stage. Have a practice session with the puppeteers. If puppets are not available, two older boys, using the tape, can do a pantomime.

On Hand

- ❏ *kids POWer hour* tape
- ❏ tape player
- ❏ *POWer house* papers
- ❏ gloves
- ❏ small prizes for joyful gloves
- ❏ larger prize for the kid's glove
- ❏ labeled jar
- ❏ posterboard
- ❏ child-sized hand cutouts
- ❏ four fluorescent flashcards
- ❏ chalkboard and chalk, or dry erase board or poster, markers
- ❏ square box covered with white paper
- ❏ newspaper for covering tables
- ❏ molding clay (recipe on page 14)
- ❏ Zip-loc bags
- ❏ pans of water
- ❏ paper towels
- ❏ box with lid labeled "Jesus"
- ❏ items important to children, *e.g.*, toys, books, candy
- ❏ basket (small enough to overflow when the items important to children are placed in it)
- ❏ copy of puppet script
- ❏ puppets
- ❏ pillows
- ❏ belts or ropes
- ❏ broom or length of rope

POWer of Worship

Welcome (6 minutes)

The Handy Helpers, wearing their joyful gloves, are stationed at the door to welcome each child and give him or her a big handshake. Each handyman and handmaiden should give the prize in his glove away before the session ends. For this first session, to acquaint children with the program and create excitement, arrange for several children to be given joyful handshakes as they enter.

If Handy Dan advertised the Hands-Full program at the last *kids POWer hour*, the children should be given cutout hands to sign and place in the appropriate jars, as they enter. The Handy Helpers need to be available to assist preschoolers and be sure that signed hands go in the right jars.

If the program has not been announced, start by welcoming the children to *kids POWer hour*. Handy Dan interrupts by staggering into the room, arms loaded with labeled jars, to give his "commercial." In this case, the children will start putting their hands in the jars at the next *kids POWer hour*.

Acknowledge birthdays and welcome guests.

Acquaint the children with the crowd control signal for this series—a rhythmic handclap. Clap your hands and have the children repeat the rhythm. Any time you give this particular handclap, they are to immediately repeat it as a sign that they are listening.

Point out the *POWer line* with the missing vowels. Ask the children to help you complete the words. When the *POWer line*, **"Walking hand in hand with Jesus pays more than it costs,"** is complete, repeat it together several times.

Sing unto the Lord (6 minutes)

Use a visualized song and the *kids POWer hour* tape to teach the theme song, "My J-O-Yful Hands." See page 94 for words and music.

Clap as you sing, "J-O-Y-F-U-L H-A-N-D-S," except on the third line where hands are raised.

J-O-Y-F-U-L H-A-N-D-S

Tune: M-I-C-K-E-Y M-O-U-S-E

J-O-Y-F-U-L H-A-N-D-S!
Joyful hands, joyful hands
Together let us raise our hands up high, high, HIGH! HIGH!
Children raise their hands higher, higher, higher.
Come along and sing this song and join the jubilee.
J-O-Y-F-U-L H-A-N-D-S!

Explain that a "jubilee" is a joyful celebration—an apt definition of *kids POWer hour*.

> **PLUG-IN** Any time the children are asked to "hold hands," the helpers should be ready to step in and fill in gaps where the children are reluctant to hold hands.

Dynamo kid specials are songs, musicals, recitations, etc. by the children. This time is designed to help them develop their talents and bring glory to God—not show off. Children look forward to this part of kids POWer hour.

Work with them to help them prepare. Give everyone a chance to shine.

As you teach children the chorus of "Hand in Hand with Jesus," explain that this is the title of our *kids POWer hour* lesson. Repeat the *POWer line*: **Walking hand in hand with Jesus pays more than it costs.**

Other fitting choruses which the children probably know are:
"Lift Up Your Hands and Praise the Lord"
"If We All Will Pull Together" (For variety, add "walk together.")
Have the children hold hands and march in place.

Allow time for one or two short Dynamo kid specials.

Lift Up Holy Hands (4 minutes)

Ask the children with Bibles to find Psalm 28:2. The simplest way is to open the Bible in the middle. They will open in the Book of Psalms or close to it. Helpers should circulate among the children, assisting as needed. Remember preschoolers love to "read along." Ask children with Bibles to share with those beside them who do not have one. Read together.

"Hear the voice of my supplications, when I cry unto thee, when I lift up my hands toward thy holy oracle."

Define supplications as *"prayers, earnest requests,"* and oracle as *"the house of the Lord."*

Why do you raise your hand in school? To get the teacher's attention. **Why do we raise our hands when we pray?** To get God's attention.

After taking "supplications," ask the children to raise their hands in God's "holy oracle." "Cry unto" the Lord in a congregation prayer. When the prayer is concluded, repeat the verse and point out how the children have obeyed it.

Hand-n-Hand Art (10 minutes)

Have paper-covered tables set up around the room. Place a lump of clay for every two children on tables with enough space between them to work comfortably.

Divide into pairs and give each a lump of clay. This activity demonstrates partnership. Each child uses only one hand to help create a sculpture. One child should be the "right hand" and the other the "left hand." Each team member has one hand behind his or her back.

After five minutes, have each pair show their "masterpiece" and everyone give them a hand. Allow time for a quick wash break.

Lead the children into a discussion of how important it was for them to work together. **It is important that we work hand in hand with Jesus, too. If we do our own thing, and do not let Jesus help us, our lives will end up in a big mess. Like our sculptures, it would have been harder to do with just one hand, but with our partner's helping hand, it was a lot easier.**

Save the clay for another activity, or divide into Zip-loc bags for children to take home.

> **Play Clay**
>
> In a saucepan, stir together 2 cups baking soda and 1 cup corn starch. Add 1 1/4 cups water. Cook over medium heat, stirring constantly, until the mixture is the consistency of moist mashed potatoes.
>
> Turn out onto a plate and cover with a damp cloth until it is cool enough to handle.
>
> Store in a plastic covered container or Zip-loc bag.

> **PLUG-IN** Testimony time is training ground for witnessing. By testifying, children learn to speak up for Jesus in front of their peers.

Speak Up for Jesus (4 minutes)

Ask the children to share a joyful event which has happened to them since the last *kids POWer hour*. It might be the addition of a new baby or pet to their family, getting a good grade on a test, receiving the Holy Ghost, etc. After each child testifies, a big round of applause should be given to the child who "witnessed" and to the Lord Jesus who gave the blessing.

Emphasize that "every good and perfect gift" comes from the hand of the Lord, although the children often receive it from the hands of their parents and friends.

From Our Hands to Yours (3 minutes)

Acquaint children with the offering project for this series and show them how it will be charted on the graph.

Play a lively tune as the children march and give.

A Lesson from the Toolbox (3 minutes)

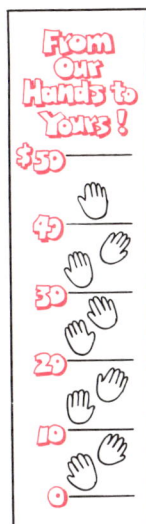

Handy Dan sits on his stool at the workbench as he gives this object lesson. **In this series, "J-O-Yful Hands," we are going to see lots of gloves.** Pull glove from toolbox. **This looks like a nice, warm work glove, doesn't it? Let's see how much work it will do.** Give glove commands like, "Shake hands with Jeremy," "Pick up this hammer." **For some reason this glove won't do anything. It just lays here. It looks like a hand. It has five "fingers."**

I guess this glove is no good. I might as well throw it away. What do you think is wrong with it? Encourage the children to respond.

Oh, you think I should put it on? Okay, let's see what happens. Put on glove and repeat commands given. **Well, what do you know—now the glove can shake Jeremy's hand and pick up this hammer. It has life because my hand is in it.**

Take off glove. **We are like this glove, flat and useless, without the Holy Ghost—God's Spirit.** Put glove back on. **But when we receive God's Spirit, we receive His power that helps us do the things we need to do! Let's always walk hand in hand with Jesus!**

POWer of the Word

From Hand to Heart (5 minutes)

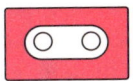 

Read together from the Bible Mark 12:29-30. Explain that memorizing God's Word moves it from our hands to our hearts.

After the children have repeated verse 29 phrase by phrase several times, move on to verse 30. As you read "with all thy heart," the children turn quickly around and face the wall with the heart flashcard on it, and so on with "soul," "mind," and "strength." When you read, "this is the first commandment," the children spin around one time and sit down. Start slowly and increase tempo each time. Let older children take turns being the leader, reading (or quoting) the verse. Use the *kids POWer hour* tape to start teaching the song, "Two Great Commandments." See page 93 for words.

Worship Chorus (2 minutes)

"Seek Ye First the Kingdom of God" would be an appropriate worship chorus at this time.

ILLUSTRATED SERMON

Make Bible characters of puppets by making robes, as shown on page 18, and pinning a length of cloth around their heads to form a turban. Peter's robe should be made of rough drab cloth. The rich young ruler's robe should be a brilliant color with gold trim.

The Rich Young Ruler and Peter (8 minutes)

Make biblical robes for puppets, as shown in the margin.

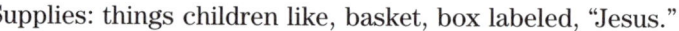

Copy the puppet script from page 17. Tape it inside the puppet stage for a guide for puppeteers to use as the *kids POWer hour* tape plays. After the riddles, the tape is turned off and the teacher interacts with the children until they solve (or do not solve) the riddle. The puppet should nod or shake his head wildly as the children call out names. He does not speak because his voice would not match the voice on the tape.

Encourage the puppeteers to use lots of puppet body language as the tape plays. Puppets should be expressive, move back and forth, wave their hands.

If puppets are not available, two boys wearing biblical robes could pantomime as the tape plays.

Room for Jesus (5 minutes)

Supplies: things children like, basket, box labeled, "Jesus."

The rich young ruler's life was full of things. Name the things as you place them in the basket. The basket should be overflowing.

Hold up the box labeled, "Jesus." **His life was so full, he had no room for Jesus. What would he have had to do to make room for Jesus?** Get rid of some "things."

When we crowd our lives with things, often there is no room for Jesus. We get so busy we forget to pray. We do not have time to come to *kids POWer hour*. We are too busy to be kind to others.

Are the things we put in the basket bad? No, they are not bad— but if things make us forget about Jesus, then they are bad for us.

Let's start our experiment over. Let's put Jesus in first. Take everything out of the basket. Then put the box in. **Is there room for anything else?** Children will probably say, "No," or "Not much." **But wait a minute. Watch.** Take off the lid and fill the box with the things.

When we put Jesus first, there is room for the things that are good for us. But we must put Him first. Explain how when we pray first, we seem to have more time; when we pay our tithes first, our money goes farther, etc.

The Needle's Eye

Read Mark 10:25 to the children. The Bible teaches that it is easier for a camel to go through a very small opening than it will be for people who are worried about their possessions to go to heaven.

Have a pillow and belt or rope for each boy. Tie pillows on their backs to make "camels." Divide into two or three camel trains.

Let the girls take turns being the gate keepers, two per gate. Have a gate for each team. The gate keepers lower a broom handle or piece of rope as the "camels" crawl through. Each time a camel crawls through, the gate keepers lower the rope or broom handle a bit more. When a camel's load touches the "gate," he is out. The camels keep going through the gate until no one can get through.

Invitation and Prayer (5-? minutes)

Musician plays. Children could stand and hum, "Hand in Hand with Jesus."
Are you walking hand in hand with Jesus? Walking with Jesus is simply obeying Him. Have you obeyed the instructions Peter gave on the Day of Pentecost?

What did he say we must do to be saved? Quote together Acts 2:38. Briefly explain how the children do this. Invite those who wish to repent or receive the Holy Ghost to the front. Emphasize the rewards of walking with Jesus.

Review

Play The Needle's Eye. Emphasize that we often must lay aside things in order to get into the kingdom of God. Smaller children may not understand this concept right now, but they will remember the game. Someday the truth of it will come to them.

Have the drawings from the Hands-Full Jars if the program started this *POWer hour*.

Give each child a *POWer house* paper.

The Rich Young Ruler and Peter

Puppets: Rich Young Ruler, Peter

ENTER RULER during musical introduction.

RULER: Looks around. **Hello, boys and girls. I know you, but I doubt if you know me. Let's see if you can guess my name. Answer this riddle.**

> **I was rich and I was young.**
> **I sinned not in word or tongue.**
> **I was a ruler and I came**
> **Running to Jesus. What's my name?**

One more time I'll say it for you. Listen carefully.

> **I was rich and I was young.**
> **I sinned not in word or tongue.**
> **I was a ruler and I came**
> **Running to Jesus. What's my name?**

Turn off the tape as the children guess.

Sorry, that's not right. I guess that wasn't fair. It really is a trick riddle because my name is not given in the Bible. And that's sad because I could have been named with Peter, James, and John. I could have been one of Jesus' disciples.

Let me tell you about myself. Now I don't want to sound like I'm boasting, but facts are facts. I was rich. I was young. I was a ruler!

I was an important young man with a lot of responsibility and lots of money. Many people looked to me for orders. I was a busy man. I was the boss.

And I was a good guy too! I didn't lie, cheat, or steal. I respected my parents. I knew that was very important.

But I wasn't happy. Something was missing. I needed Jesus. Runs in place. **So I went running to Him, eager to hear what He would tell me.** Bows. **I fell down at His feet and asked, "What must I do to inherit eternal life?"**

JESUS: Background. **One thing is missing in your life. Go, sell what you have, and give your money to the poor. Follow me. Be My disciple and you will have treasure in heaven.**

RULER: Shocked. **I couldn't believe my ears. Sell what I had? How could Jesus ask me to sell what I had? Didn't He know that I had lots and lots of things?**

Nods sadly. **Yes, Jesus knew. And He knew that my things had me, too. I loved things—too much—more than I loved God.**

Jesus also knew that I loved being the boss. I didn't want to give that up to obey someone else—not even Jesus. I was not willing to give up my things and my position to walk hand in hand with Jesus.

Starts to exit. **So I turned and walked slowly away. And that's why no one knows my name. In the end I lost all my things *and* my hope of eternal life. I didn't realize that it pays more to walk with Jesus than it costs.**

EXIT RULER.

ENTER PETER during musical interlude.

PETER: **Praise the Lord! Didn't you hear me? I said, "Praise the Lord."** Brief pause waiting for children's response. Louder. **I can't hear you. I said, "Praise the Lord!"** Brief pause. **That was a little better, but you can do much better. One more time—everybody say, "Praise the Lord!"** Pause. **That's great!**

It's my turn to ask you a riddle. Let's see if you can guess my name.

> **I followed Jesus everywhere He went.**
> **To fish for men I was sent.**
> **On the Day of Pentecost I preached the Word**
> **And over three thousand souls were stirred.**
> **What's my name?**

Turn off tape as children guess.

You got it! My name is Peter. I had the opportunity to walk with Jesus, and I took it. It was the best decision I ever made.

I was a fisherman, in business with my brother Andrew. One day Jesus called to us.

JESUS: Background. **Follow me, and I will make you fishers of men.**

PETER: Now Jesus' offer sounded a lot better than fishing for fish. So Andrew and I left our fishing business and followed Jesus.

During the time I followed Jesus I saw many miracles. I even performed a few. In Jesus' name I healed the sick and raised the dead. Wow! That was exciting!

As I walked with Jesus, some of my friends walked away, like the rich young ruler that was just here. Sure it costs something to follow Jesus. I walked away from my fishing business—gave up the right to be my own boss. I let Jesus be the boss. I went where He told me and did what He said. That's what walking with Jesus is—obeying His Word, letting Him be the boss. I knew if I stayed with Him, I would have treasure in heaven.

Let me tell you about a sermon I preached to some people who asked what they had to do to walk with Jesus. You can find it in Acts the second chapter.

It was on the Day of Pentecost after I received the Holy Ghost. Quote Acts 2:38 with me right now. Preach it! *"Repent, and be baptized every one of you in the name of Jesus Christ for the remission of sins, and ye shall receive the gift of the Holy Ghost."*

That message is for you. If you will repent of your sins, and be baptized in Jesus' name, you can receive the Holy Ghost and walk with Jesus. And you'll discover that *it pays more than it costs to walk with Jesus.*

EXIT PETER during musical finale.

PERMISSION TO COPY SCRIPT

Fold length of cloth in half; cut a hole for the opening.

stitch or glue sides

STITCH OR GLUE EDGES

cut Two

Sing unto the Lord

Did you ever notice that a child sings with his whole being? It is hard for a singing child to sit still. He claps, stomps, dances, twists, bounces. Singing is not something we do just with our voices.

Singing saturates the soul.

Sing action-filled songs in *kids POWer hour*. In this series special emphasis is given to the hands. Let the children do motions, clap, raise their hands in praise, play rhythm band instruments (kitchen utensils will do).

Make visualized songs on posterboard, cut into shapes related to the song. To preserve, laminate. Let children use their hands to hold these visuals as the class sings.

Unit One
Basic Truths

Unit Aim: To give children basics for developing a relationship with Jesus Christ.

Memory Passage: Mark 12:29-30

J=Jesus First
O=Others Second
Y=You Last

Heart in Hand

Scripture Text: Luke 7:36-48

When we love Jesus, we worship with our hearts and serve with our hands.

 **Shop Talk**

✓ Does Handy Dan know what is expected of him? Go over the program together.
✓ Gather supplies. Fill the joyful gloves and the kid's glove.
✓ Use this rebus as a pattern to make a large poster of the *POWer line*. Display in front of the room.

✓ For the review game, "Follow Your Heart," cut out a supply of red paper hearts. On each write a simple instruction such as you would give in the game, "Mother, May I?"—take two rabbit hops, take three baby steps, take one giant step, take one kangaroo leap, crawl forward two steps, etc.
✓ On three index cards, write out Psalm 24:3, Psalm 24:4, and Psalm 24:5. Before the service give these to three readers to read aloud.
✓ Add review questions to your notebook.
✓ For each six to eight children, cover a box with white paper. Write, "heart," "soul," "mind," and "strength" on four sides. Add symbols to aid non-readers. On the remaining two sides write, "Mark 12:29-30."
✓ Each child will need a construction paper heart and pencil for the Heart-n-Hand activity. Draw a bare tree on a poster or "plant" a dead branch in a bucket.
✓ The Illustrated Sermon is given as a pantomime by a

Schedule

Date: _____

I. POWer of Worship (25-30 minutes)
  A. Welcome (5 minutes)
    • Hands-Full Jar
    • Three POWerful Words
    • Announcements
  B. Sing unto the Lord (6 minutes)
    • Rhythm Band
    • Dynamo Specials
  C. A Lesson from the Toolbox (5 minutes)
    • Give God a Handle
  D. Lift Up Holy Hands (4 minutes)
    • Psalm 24:3-5
  E. Heart-n-Hand (8 minutes)
    • Praising God's Children
  F. From Our Hands to Yours (3 minutes)
II. POWer of the Word (25-30 minutes)
  A. From Hand to Heart (8 minutes)
    • Roll the Cube
  B. Worship Chorus (2 minutes)
  C. Illustrated Sermon (6 minutes)
    • Pantomime: The Woman Who Anointed Jesus' Feet
  D. Hand Washing (8 minutes)
  E. Invitation and Prayer (5-? minutes)
  F. Review Game
    • Follow Your Heart

On Hand

- ☐ *kids POWer hour* tape
- ☐ tape player
- ☐ *POWer house* papers
- ☐ labeled jars
- ☐ child's hand cutouts
- ☐ gloves and prizes
- ☐ rhythm band instruments or kitchen utensils
- ☐ poster of bare tree or dead branch planted in a bucket
- ☐ Plasti-Tak
- ☐ chalkboard and chalk or dry erase board and markers
- ☐ biblical robes
- ☐ flashlight
- ☐ decorative container
- ☐ basin of water (one for each six or eight children)
- ☐ towel (one for each six or eight children)
- ☐ sponge (one for each six or eight children)
- ☐ kiwi and knife (optional)

"woman" and "Simon" as the *kids POWer hour* tape plays. (If you do not have the tape, record Luke 7:36-39, 44-48.) With a little practice, two older children, dressed in biblical robes can play these roles.

✓ Check the Plug In on page 22. You might want to start using the volunteer jar this *POWer hour*.

✓ Meet early with your staff for prayer.

POWer of Worship

Welcome (5 minutes)

As the children enter, have handymen and handmaidens, wearing joyful gloves, stationed beside work tables at the door to help the children with the Hands-Full Jar activity.

Handy Dan, carrying his toolbox containing a Bible, greets as many children by name as possible, visits with them a few seconds, and asks if they have anything that needs fixed. If a child confides in him a need for prayer, he can pray with the child right then. He may even ask other children to join in a prayer circle. If a Bible verse will help, he gives an index card with an appropriate verse on it to the child. If the need is intense, he should pass the information on to the pastor. Handy Dan should be sensitive to the Holy Ghost as he visits with the children.

Give the clap you developed last *POWer hour* to remind the children of the crowd control signal. They should repeat the clap, matching the beat.

On a board in front of the class put these lines.

___   ___ ___ ___ ___   ___ ___ ___

Announce that the Handy Helpers will be listening for the three most POWerful words in the world. Clue: they fit on these blanks. The first child to say these POWerful words will be given the kid's glove to wear. (See page 6 for instruction on the kid's glove.)

Greet visitors, congratulate birthday children, and make announcements. Ask the children to read together the *POWer line* from the rebus poster. **When we love Jesus, we worship with our hearts and serve with our hands.**

Sing unto the Lord (6 minutes)

Give each child a simple rhythm band instrument. Allow times for only instruments or only voices. If instruments are not available, use your imagination to produce "j-o-yful" noise-makers—dried beans in a plastic container, pots and pans played with spoons, whistles, anything that could shake, rattle, or roll! This is a high-energy activity. When finished, to bring the noise and excitement level down, have the children whisper or hum a song as they march around, putting the musical instruments in a storage box.

Have one or two Dynamo specials.

A Lesson from the Toolbox (5 minutes)

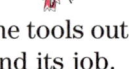

Handy Dan comes to the front, lugging his toolbox. He pulls the tools out one by one and asks the children if they can identify each tool and its job.

Now I have a riddle for you. Even though these tools look different and perform different tasks, they all have one thing. What is it? Allow the children to guess. **Each tool has a handle, a place for the hand that uses them.**

We are like tools, ready to be used by God, except we do not have a handle. We have to give ourselves to God in order for Him to use us.

When we do good deeds, we are letting God use us. Give God a handle on your life by being willing to help others.

Lift Up Holy Hands (4 minutes)

Ask preassigned readers to stand and read Psalm 24:3-5.

After the Scripture reading, Handy Dan shows the children his stained, dirty hands, explaining that fixing things is dirty work. He expresses fear that he cannot "stand in the presence of the Lord" because his hands are not clean. He asks the reader of Psalm 24:4 to read it again. He continues to interact as the director explains.

"Clean hands" in this verse does not mean clean fingernails and scrubbed knuckles. It means we have not done dirty, underhanded things. Often people accused of wrong doing will deny their guilt by saying, "My hands are clean." To have clean hands is to be innocent.

No one can say, "I have never done wrong." The Bible tells us that "all have sinned." Spiritually, everyone has dirty hands.

When you get your hands dirty at play or work, what do you do?

When we do wrong and get our hands dirty spiritually, we can wash them by asking God to forgive us. Repentance washes our hands clean and gives us the right to stand in the presence of God.

Ask the children to bow their heads and lead them in a simple prayer of repentance.

Take prayer requests and ask one of your helpers to lead in a congregational prayer. Conclude by asking everyone to "lift up clean hands" in praise and thanksgiving to God for answering their prayers.

Heart-n-Hand (8 minutes)

Give each child a construction paper heart and pencil. Ask them to write on it something nice about the person on their right. (If seated in rows, the last child in the row writes about the first child.) Handymen and handmaidens should assist as needed and control negative comments.

Explain that this testimony time will be given to "praising God's kids." One by one the children come to the front, share their "heart," and add it to the tree. Point out the difference "loving words" made in the tree.

What are some ways we can express our love? By doing kind things. **That is how we put a handle on our love like Handy Dan suggested.**

From Our Hands to Yours (3 minutes)

Quickly find the first book of the New Testament. For preschoolers point out the dividing page between the Old and New Testaments.

Now find Matthew 6. Ask the girls to stand and read verse 3, then the boys to stand and read verse 4. Explain that *alms* means "offering."

Handy Dan becomes perplexed and tries to figure out how he can give with his right hand without his left hand knowing how much he is giving because his "brain always tells on him." He should go through exaggerated motions trying to turn off his brain so he can give without his left hand knowing what he is doing.

> Handy Dan interacts with the director, as needed, to explain "clean hands" to the children.

> During prayer time would be a good time to hear a child say the secret, POWerful words, "I love you." Handymen and handmaidens should be listening.

> Nothing pleases a father more than hearing nice things said about his children. Vary the testimony service by asking the children to "praise" one another.

> Again Handy Dan interacts with the director, this time to clarify the meaning of Matthew 6:3-4.
> Or for variety, use a puppet for Handy Dan's part.

Volunteer Jar

This is a system for choosing participants for activities or asking questions. Write names on one end of a wooden tongue depressor or craft stick. As the occasion arises, choose a stick. When that child has participated, turn his name upside down in the jar. When all have been turned, start again.

The director explains. **Give quietly and without a big show. Do not brag about what you are giving, and God will reward you.**

Handy Dan says he is glad to know that because there doesn't seem to be any way to turn off his brain without going to sleep. And how could he give if he was asleep?

Let the children march and sing the theme song, "My J-O-Yful Hands," as they give. Record the offering total on the graph.

POWer of the Word

From Hand to Heart (8 minutes)

Sing "Two Great Commandments," using the *kids POWer hour* tape.

Write Mark 12:29-30 on a board, having the children read aloud as you write. Read together several times, then erase.

Divide into circles of six or eight children. A helper or older child should be the leader of each group. Give each group a labeled box. Sitting in a circle, the children take turns rolling the cube. If "strength" is up, the child tells how he can love the Lord with all his strength, etc. If the reference side is turned up, the child (or team) quotes the verse. Some prompting may be required.

Teach the song, "Love the Lord," using the *kids POWer hour* tape. Transparency master is on page 95.

Worship Chorus (2 minutes)

Sing a slow, worship chorus such as, "Hand in Hand with Jesus."

ILLUSTRATED SERMON

The Woman Who Anointed Jesus' Feet (6 minutes)

Repeat together the *POWer line*. **Our Bible story is about a lady who showed Jesus the love in her heart by what she brought in her hands.**

Set up a table with two chairs beside it. Simon sits in one. The woman kneels in front of the other.

Lights are dimmed. As the *kids POWer hour* tape recording of Luke 7:36-39, 44-48 (paraphrased) plays, the players pantomime the actions. A flashlight spotlights the players during their parts. For Jesus, shine the light on the floor as no one plays His role. A copy of the reading is given here for a guide.

ENTER SIMON, sits at the table.
NARRATOR: **Now one of the Pharisees invited Jesus to have dinner with him, so he went to the Pharisee's house and reclined at the table.**
ENTER WOMAN, carrying decorative container. She stands behind the empty

chair, weeping. As the text is read, she moves around in front of the chair and kneels, making appropriate motions.

NARRATOR: **When a woman who had lived a sinful life in that town learned that Jesus was eating at the Pharisee's house, she brought an alabaster jar of perfume, and as she stood behind Him at His feet weeping, she began to wet His feet with her tears. Then she wiped them with her hair, kissed them, and poured perfume on them.**
When the Pharisee who had invited Him saw this, he said to himself. . . .

SIMON: Microphone on reverb. *If this man were a prophet, He would know who is touching Him and what kind of woman she is—that she is a sinner.*

NARRATOR: **Then [Jesus] turned toward the woman and said to Simon. . . .**

JESUS: **Do you see this woman? I came into your house. You did not give Me any water for My feet, but she wet My feet with her tears and wiped them with her hair. You did not give Me a kiss, but this woman, from the time I entered, has not stopped kissing My feet. You did not put oil on My head, but she has poured perfume on My feet.**
Therefore, I tell you, her many sins have been forgiven—for she loved much. But he who has been forgiven little loves little. Simon looks sorrowful.
Woman, your sins are forgiven.

Woman bows head to ground while lights go out. SIMON and WOMAN EXIT.

(paraphrase of Luke 7:36-39, 44-48)

PERMISSION TO COPY SCRIPT

How did this woman show her love for Jesus? Let the children discuss.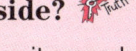
When we love Jesus, we worship with our hearts and serve with our hands.

During Bible times people usually walked everywhere they went, so they washed their feet frequently. When they entered a house, it was the servant's job to wash the guest's feet. If there were no servants, the host would do it.

Simon invited Jesus to his house, but he did not show Him the courtesy of washing His feet. The woman, a stranger, did this task for Jesus. How did Jesus reward her for washing His feet? He forgave her sins. **Simon chose not to serve Jesus and he missed a blessing.**

This Is the Way We Wash Our Hands (8 minutes)

While the mood of the class is quiet, have the children move into circles of six to eight. Provide a basin of clean, warm water, a sponge, and a towel for each circle.

Let's worship the Lord the way the woman did. We serve others with our hands. Let's leave here today with clean hands to go and serve others. God wants to use us to serve.

Gently wash the hands of the first person in the circle with the sponge and dry with a towel. That child then washes the hands of the child next to him and so on.

Invitation and Prayer (5-? minutes)

The music plays softly. With the children still in circles, invite them to dedicate their hands and hearts to the Lord. Emphasize that because of the love in Jesus' heart, He allowed His hands to be pierced at Calvary for our sins.

Optional

What's on the Inside?

Hold up a kiwi. Pass it around.

This may look strange and ugly, but the inside is completely different. Cut open the kiwi, showing the bright green pulp.

Many people judge others by what they look like on the outside. Simon did this to the woman in our lesson. We found out that her heart was soft toward Jesus.

Some people may ask, "What could a child do for Jesus?" There are many ways you can serve Jesus because your hearts are soft. That means you are not mean and uncaring.

Let's see how many ways we can name that children can serve the Lord. Write the ways on a board as the children name them.

> Make arrangements ahead of time so there will be order during the altar service. The music director could lead those who are not praying in worship choruses. Or some of the helpers could take the sincere seekers to another room to pray.

When we love Jesus, we worship with our hearts and serve with our hands.

Ask those who love Jesus in their hearts to stand and raise their hands as a sign that they will serve Him.

Lead the children in a prayer of dedication. Handymen and handmaidens should be scattered around the room ready to pray with the children.

Review

Players line up along one wall of the room to play Follow Your Heart.

Ask a player a review question. If he answers correctly, he draws a paper heart and follows the instructions on it, such as, "take one giant step." If a child misses a question, he stays where he is. The first player to reach the opposite wall or finish line is the winner.

If no one said the secret, POWerful words, tell the children that the words were "I love you." Encourage them to use these words often in the coming week and watch what happens.

Have the drawing from the Hands-Full Jars.

Distribute the *POWer house* papers as the children leave.

Puppet Spectacular continued from p. 11

Think about taking your puppet ministry outside the four walls of the church. Nursing homes are excellent places to have a puppet show. The residents are appreciative and complimentary, and your puppeteers will benefit from the positive feedback. It also gives you extra practice before an uncritical audience. Other possibilities are hospitals, malls, and backyard Sunday schools. Some puppet teams support their puppet ministry by performing at special events such as birthday parties. Proceeds go to buy puppets and equipment.

There are many props and special effects you can use. Black lights are effective, as are backdrops attached to the back of the puppet stage. Props are necessities. You can attach them to rods and have a puppeteer work the props. The props are especially useful if you only have a few, inexpensive puppets. Patterns are available for building handy, simple prop racks.

In addition:

1. Start a file of puppet catalogs. These are full of good ideas.
2. Subscribe to a puppet newsletter. *The Son Shine Gazette* is published quarterly by The Son Shine Puppet Company, P. O. Box 6203, Rockford, IL 61125. One Way Street also publishes a newsletter, *One Way Street News*. Write One Way Street, Inc., P. O. Box 5077, Englewood, CO 80155 and ask to be put on their mailing list. Or call 303-790-1188.
3. Attend puppet workshops.
4. Catalog puppet tapes and keep a master copy.
5. Build a library of puppet books.

How can I use puppets in *kids POWer hour* and Sunday school?

The possibilities are endless:

1. Puppets can greet children, make announcements, give instructions, take attendance, teach appropriate behavior.
2. Teach a new song, or sing a song to accent lesson.
3. Teach or review a memory verse.
4. Introduce the lesson.
5. Teach the lesson, or reinforce the application of the lesson. Use the same puppet or group of puppets each week to whet the children's interest about the lesson. We used three puppets every Sunday for one quarter to talk about the main theme of each lesson. We had a bad guy, Granny (a Christian), and a guy who tried to ride the fence. Granny ran the bad guy out of town every week by quoting the Bible verse. After a few Sundays the children began to quote Scriptures every time the bad guy showed up.
6. Express feelings, discuss special problems.
7. Review lessons.

Unit One
Basic Truths

Unit Aim: To give children basics for developing a relationship with Jesus Christ.

Memory Passage: Mark 12:29-30

Open Hands

J = Jesus First
O = Others Second
Y = You Last

Scripture Text: Mark 12:41-44

 When we give all, it is much.

Shop Talk

✓ Make copies of the *POWer house* papers and enough funny money that each child can be given a generous share. Or purchase play money. Put two pennies in a coin purse.

✓ Handy Dan needs a plumb line for his toolbox lesson.

✓ A Scrabble™ game or one with letter tiles is needed to introduce the lesson topic.

✓ Make five fluorescent flashcards—G I V E R.

✓ For the Hand-n-Glove skit you need several different types of gloves, such as rubber or surgical, winter, leather, fancy, cellophane, fluorescent hunting gloves. One puppeteer is needed for each pair. Use a simple puppet stage large enough to accommodate several puppeteers. A sheet stretched across a corner will do. Let children who are not normally used in puppet skits participate. A short practice session is required.

✓ Cover a box with gold foil. Add a trumpet or funnel-shape to the top. Cut a hole in the lid so the money dropped into the funnel will fall into the box.

✓ For the review game number nine envelopes. In six envelopes place a slip of paper saying, "Sorry." In the other three place a paper saying, "You're a winner." Tack or tape these to the wall in a tic-tac-toe grid. For a large group or if you usually have a long time for review games, make a larger grid.

Schedule
Date: _____

I. POWer of Worship (25-30 minutes)
   A. Welcome (8 minutes)
      • Hands-Full Jars
      • Opening Prayer
      • Un-Scramble the *POWer line*
      • Announcements
   B. Sing unto the Lord (6 minutes)
      • Praise Choruses
      • Dynamo Specials
   C. Lift Up Holy Hands (5 minutes)
      • Psalm 134:2—A Praise Break
      • Prayer Requests
   D. Hand-n-Glove Puppet Skit (5 minutes)
   E. From Our Hands to Yours (5 minutes)
      • Tight-fisted or Open-handed?
   F. Stand Up for Jesus (3 minutes)
      • Hand Picked
II. POWer of the Word (25-30 minutes)
   A. From Hand to Heart (5 minutes)
      • Mark 12:29-30
   B. Worship Chorus (2 minutes)
   C. A Lesson from the Toolbox (5 minutes)
      • The Plumb line
   D. Illustrated Sermon (8 minutes)
      • The Widow's Mite
   E. Invitation and Prayer (5-? minutes)
   F. Review
      • Pick an Envelope

On Hand

❏ *kids POWer hour* tape
❏ tape player
❏ *POWer house* papers
❏ Scrabble™ game
❏ plumb line
❏ fluorescent posterboard
❏ joyful and kid's gloves
❏ small prizes
❏ several coins
❏ variety of gloves
❏ funny or play money
❏ two pennies
❏ coin purse
❏ drab, ragged biblical robe and scarf
❏ gold foil covered box for offering
❏ nine envelopes
❏ hard wrapped candies

Decide beforehand the criteria for wearing the kid's glove. It could be the child who brings the most visitors, has the next birthday, etc.

Note This

During this series the children are learning several new words, *oracle, supplications, sanctuary, alms*. Include these in the review questions in your notebook.

POWer of Worship

Welcome (8 minutes)

Handymen and handmaidens, wearing joyful gloves, shake hands with everyone and occasionally surprise a child with a "joyful handshake."

They help the children register for the Hands-Full Jar drawings. Before the children can put a hand in the Recited Memory Passage jar, they must quote Mark 12:29-30. It is doubtful that anyone will be able to do this at the beginning of the *POWer hour* so these may be added during the memory work session.

Again Handy Dan welcomes the children and "fixes broken things," like feelings. Any job too big for him, he gives to the Master Carpenter, by praying with the child.

At starting time, give the crowd control clap. Then ask the children to bow their heads and lead in a simple opening prayer.

Scatter the letter tiles from a Scrabble™ game in the center of a table, letters facing up. Choose two teams of two readers. They can represent boys versus girls, right side of room versus left, whatever. Position a team at each end of the table. Have the group repeat the *POWer line* after you several times.

When we give all, it is much.

The goal is to see which team can spell out the *POWer line* first using the letter tiles. The audience can repeat the *POWer line* as needed to help their team.

Give both teams a round of applause. Tell the children that each time you give the crowd control clap they are to shout out the *POWer line*.

Make announcements, welcome guests, and acknowledge birthdays.

Sing unto the Lord (6 minutes)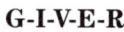

G-I-V-E-R
Tune: B-I-N-G-O
**G-I-V-E-R, G-I-V-E-R, G-I-V-E-R
I will be a giver !**

Vary the song by singing in slow motion, speeding up each time. Or vary the volume.

Give flashcards, G I V E R, to five children, who, as their letter is sung, step out, and hold it above their heads. At the end of the song, children give their card to someone else.

Sing "If You're Happy and You Know it, Clap Your Hands." Try doing the actions with closed fists. Point out you can only clap with open hands!

Allow time for a Dynamo Special or two.

Lift Up Holy Hands (5 minutes)

"Lift up your hands in the sanctuary, and bless the LORD" (Psalm 134:2). Quote this verse several times, having the children repeat it after you at varied volumes.

Define sanctuary. Then lead the children in a praise break as everyone lifts up his hands in the sanctuary and blesses the Lord.

Take prayer requests. Let the children with needs line up in the front. Handymen and handmaidens can gather around and lay hands on these children as they feel led. The congregation should stretch out their hands toward these children as they pray for them.

Hand-n-Glove Skit (5 minutes)

Revise this script to fit the gloves you have available.

ENTER GLOVES, chatting noisily. The narrator stands outside the stage and conducts an informal conversation with them concerning their appropriate uses. Dialogue could go something like the one here.

RUBBER: **I am very important. I protect the hand from harsh chemicals, germs, and dirt.**

LEATHER: **Hey! I like to get dirty! I'm a hard workin' guy, and everyone knows there's nothing wrong with that!**

DRESS: **Yes, but you could never go into a fine restaurant, looking like that! I could teach you a lesson or two!**

WINTER: **But I provide warmth. How could you keep a hand warm wearing silk?**

HUNTING: **When I am worn, everyone takes notice!**

NARRATOR: **Wait! Stop! You all are useful. That's what makes you special. Each of you has different abilities and ways to give. The important thing is that you give—in the best way you know how and do it to the very best of your ability. Now shake hands and let's be friends!**

Gloves shake hands. EXIT.

Have the children shake hands with three people around them while the puppeteers are returning to their seats.

PERMISSION TO COPY SCRIPT

From Our Hands to Yours (5 minutes)

Grip several coins in your hand. Call a child to the front. Tell him that you want to give him something. Try to open your fist, but pretend that it is "locked up tight."

How can I give if my fist is clinched shut? I can't. In order to give, I must open my hand. Sometimes people are called, "tight-fisted." What does this mean? They are stingy.

Let the first child to find Psalm 104:28, stand and read it.

In this verse is God's hand open or closed? What is in His hand? Are you tight-fisted or open-handed?

Open your hand and give the money to the child. Point out that for him to receive what you are giving, he had to open his hand.

A tight fist can neither give nor receive. Let's open our hands and give an offering to the Lord. We may be surprised by what He will give us in return.

Play a lively tune as the children march around singing to give their offering. God loves cheerful givers. Make giving a happy time.

Stand Up for Jesus (3 minutes)

For testimony service, hand pick as many children as you have time. Do this by walking among the children and laying your hand gently on the shoulders of the ones you choose.

Remember to give the crowd control clap at various intervals to keep the *POWer line* in the children's minds.

As you do this, talk about how God has "hand picked" each child, not just a few, to do a special work for Him. They may not know now what that work is, but when the time is right, God will show them His plan for their lives.

If there is enough time, continue randomly choosing the children until you have hand picked everyone.

Let them line up and use the microphone to testify.

POWer of the Word

> Drawing an imaginary line to divide into teams can be lots of fun. Give one end of the line to a helper. Have him move to the back of the room opposite you. The children will probably see the line better than you do.

From Hand to Heart (5 minutes)

Ask the children to find Mark 12:29-30. Read together. Then sing "Two Great Commandments," and "Love the Lord."

Call four kids to the front to be "heart," "soul," "mind," and "strength." Line them up in the proper order. The class reads the verse again. When they come to the words, "heart," "soul," "mind," and "strength," the children given that title, call out the word.

Have class close their eyes while the four scramble their order. Ask for a volunteer to come forward and say the verse, putting the children back in the proper order. If no one has memorized these verses yet, ask for a volunteer to put the children in the proper order as the class reads or sings the verses.

Repeat as often as time allows. Allow those who have memorized this passage to add their hand to the Recited Memory Passage jar.

Worship Chorus (2 minutes)

Sing a worship chorus to quieten the children's spirits and prepare their hearts for the Word of the Lord. After singing it through one time, ask the children to bow their heads, close their eyes, and hum it.

A Lesson from the Toolbox (5 minutes)

As the children sing, Handy Dan gets up from his work bench, pulls a plumb line from his toolbox, and begins checking the walls. When the singing is over, ask him what in the world he has and what he is doing.

A dialogue between the director and Handy Dan should bring out these points.

- A plumb line is basically a weight and a string.
- Handymen have been using this tool for a long time. A plumb line is even mentioned in the Old Testament! (Read Amos 7:7.)
- A plumb line is used when a wall is being built to make sure it stands straight and tall.

What would happen if the walls of our houses were crooked?

God has a plumb line too. It's the Bible. While we are building our lives, we can read in His Word to see if we measure up—if we are doing things correctly. If we are off a little on something, God's plumb line, the Bible, shows us how to get straight.

God has a plan for every area of our lives. In the Bible story we will use God's plumb line to see if we are giving God's way.

ILLUSTRATED SERMON

The Widow's Mites (8 minutes)

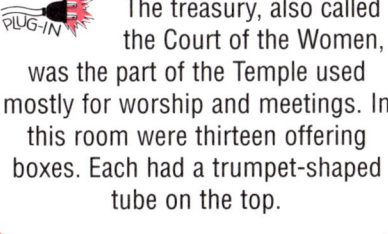

The treasury, also called the Court of the Women, was the part of the Temple used mostly for worship and meetings. In this room were thirteen offering boxes. Each had a trumpet-shaped tube on the top.

Choose one girl to be the "widow." Put a drab, ragged biblical robe on over her clothes. She can drape a scarf over her shoulders or head. Give her the coin purse with two pennies in it. Have her sit in the back until her part is read.

Number the remainder of the group, "1-2-1-2-1-2." If you have a large group, simply draw an imaginary line down the middle. Children in group 1 are the disciples; those in group 2 are the rich people. Give each rich person a generous supply of funny or play money. (For a large group limit the rich to six or eight children and the disciples to twelve. The rest are observers.)

Display the gold foil covered offering box.

Show the children how to find Mark 12:41 in their Bibles. Have the "rich" read it aloud.

"And Jesus sat over against the treasury, and beheld how the people cast money into the treasury: and many that were rich cast in much."

Jesus was sitting in the Temple watching the people give. Many rich people came and proudly cast in their offering. How do you think these people acted when they gave? Do you think they wanted other people to see how much they were giving? Why? Let children discuss. Call for the "rich" to come forward and give part of their money. Encourage them to be dramatic show-offs.

In last *kids POWer hour* we learned what Jesus said about giving. It had to do with right hands and left hands. Does anyone remember what He said? Not to let your left hand know what your right hand was giving. If the children do not remember, ask Handy Dan. **What does this mean?** Not to be a show-off. **Apparently, these rich people had not heard Jesus' teaching on giving. Or if they had heard, they were not obeying.**

Read verse 42. *"And there came a certain poor widow, and she threw in two mites, which make a farthing."*

Call the widow to come and give her offering. As she takes the pennies out of her coin purse and drops them in the offering box, point out that it is all she has. **A mite was the smallest coin in Jesus' day, much like a penny to us. It was not much at all, but it was all she had.**

Have the disciples read verse 43. *"And he called unto him his disciples, and saith unto them, Verily I say unto you, That this poor widow hath cast more in, than all they which have cast into the treasury."*

Now wait a minute, Jesus. Are You saying that this widow's two little mites are more than all the money the rich people gave? How could two pennies be more than many, many dollars? That doesn't make sense . . . or does it?

Everyone reads aloud verse 44. *"For all they did cast in of their abundance; but she of her want did cast in all that she had, even all her living."*

Jesus praised this lady and said she had given more than anyone else because they gave "some" of what they had. She gave "all."

Give crowd control clap. When we give all, it is much.

God goes not look at what we give, but what we have left. He is not concerned about how much we give, but how we give it.

Let's close our eyes just for a moment and think about the plumb line that Handy Dan showed us. Let's imagine that it is God's plumb line for giving. How do you measure up in His directions for giving? When you give, whether it be money, time, or kind deeds, are you giving to impress others or because you love the Lord?

Invitation and Prayer (5-? minutes)

Music plays softly. "All He Wants Is You," would be an appropriate chorus to sing as the altar call is made.

What does Jesus want us to give Him more than anything else— more than our money, more than our strength, more than our time? Our lives. He wants you—all of you.

When you give yourself to Jesus, you will give Him your money, your time, your strength. Does Jesus need your money? your time? your strength? No—He doesn't really need you, but He wants you because He loves you.

When you give yourself to Jesus, you are doing yourself a big favor. You are turning all your problems, your fears, your worries over to Him. When you belong to Him, He will take care of you.

Invite the children who want to give their lives to Jesus to the front to pray. This can include children who have never prayed and those who need to rededicate their lives.

Review

Divide into teams of two to four. Take turns asking each team a question. Team members should confer before answering as they only get one answer per team. If their answer is correct, they choose an envelope off the tic-tac-toe grid. If they pick a winner, give each team member a piece of wrapped candy. To keep the suspense high, players should not know how many envelopes contain winners.

Have the Hands-Full Jar drawing.

Give each child a *POWer house* paper as he leaves.

Unit One
Basic Truths

Unit Aim: To give children basics for developing a relationship with Jesus Christ.

Memory Passage: Mark 12:29-30

Near at Hand

J = Jesus First
O = Others Second
Y = You Last

Scripture Text: Luke 24:13-35; Philippians 4:5

 Jesus is always with us. We can talk to Him any time.

 Shop Talk

✓ Handy Dan needs to make his new-fangled communication device—two unopened cans with a 4'-5' string taped to each end. The director needs two empty tin cans connected with a string the length of the room tied through a hole in the end of each.

✓ Arrange for someone who knows sign language to teach a simple song and/or the memory passage Mark 12:29-30 to the children.

✓ Make a sample Braille message. Layer four sheets of typing paper. Place on a soft surface. With the tip of a pen punch out, "Jesus." Turn the pages over to feel the code. **Note:** you are punching the word backwards so it will be right when the page is turned over. Pass these four samples around. For a large group make more.

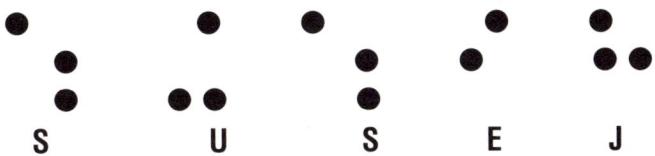

✓ Study Unit Two page and schedule a staff meeting to plan your activities for the next four *kids POWer hours.*

✓ Have prayer with your staff. Is everyone praying for *kids POWer hour* during the week? Agree together for special needs your children have.

Schedule

Date: _____

I. POWer of Worship (25-30 minutes)
  A. Welcome (8 minutes)
     • Hands-Full Jars
     • A Lesson from the Toolbox
     • Announcements
  B. Sing unto the Lord (6 minutes)
     • Sign Language
     • Dynamo Specials
  C. Getting the Message Across (5-6 minutes)
     • A Communication Sandwich
  D. Lift Up Holy Hands (5 minutes)
     • Communicating with God
  E. Pretzel Prayers (4 minutes)
  F. From Our Hands to Yours (2 minutes)
II. POWer of the Word (25-30 minutes)
  A. From Hand to Heart (5 minutes)
     • Signing Mark 12:29-30
  B. Worship Chorus (2 minutes)
  C. Illustrated Sermon (10 minutes)
     • Body Language Demonstration
     • Disciples on the Road to Emmaus
  D. Invitation and Prayer (5-? minutes)
  E. Review Game
     • Did You Get the Message?

On Hand

- ❏ *kids POWer hour* tape
- ❏ tape player
- ❏ *POWer house* papers
- ❏ Hands-Full Jars
- ❏ small prizes
- ❏ review notebook
- ❏ joyful gloves and kid's glove
- ❏ jar of pennies for grand prize drawing
- ❏ four tin cans, two opened and two unopened
- ❏ string
- ❏ note paper
- ❏ sandwich bread, peanut butter, jelly
- ❏ table knife
- ❏ twist pretzels
- ❏ small soft ball

POWer of Worship

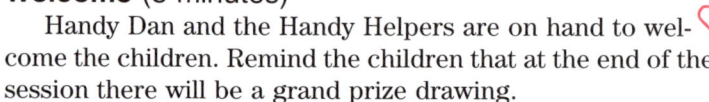

Welcome (8 minutes)

Handy Dan and the Handy Helpers are on hand to welcome the children. Remind the children that at the end of the session there will be a grand prize drawing.

As children are seated, Handy Dan takes a "new-fangled" device, a tin can communicator, from his toolbox.

HANDY DAN: **Howdy kids!** Waits for a response. **I've been fixing things for you, now I've got a problem! Do you think you could help me? I heard I could make a telephone out of tin cans and string! Now, I thought that would be a dandy idea, since the pastor is always calling on me to fix something. Why, I could rig one of these up in his office and all he'd have to do would be pick up his end and call. I'd answer real quick like.** Pulls two unopened cans connected with a string out of his toolbox. **Well, here it is. But for some reason, I can't get it to work.** Talks into the end of one can letting the kids hold the other end.

DIRECTOR: **Say, Brother Handy Dan, I think I can help you. You see, you have the right things to make a telephone, but you are using un-opened cans. Nothing can get through!** Pulls out two empty cans with strings run through a hole punched in each end and tied. **Here, try this one.**

HANDY DAN: Talks into one end, making sure the string is taut with the director holding other end across the room. **Hello? Is anybody there?**

DIRECTOR: **Yes, I read you loud and clear! See, Brother Dan, you've got to keep the lines of communication open! We're going to be talking about communication today, so we have already learned a good lesson from your problem. Thank you.**

HANDY DAN: Takes a bow. **You are most welcome.** Takes a seat among the children.

PERMISSION TO COPY SCRIPT

Make announcements, welcome guests, and acknowledge birthdays.

Sing unto the Lord (6 minutes)

Have someone who knows sign language teach the children how to sign a simple song. Emphasize that they can sign with their hands what is in their hearts.

Lead the children in a couple of choruses from the *kids POWer hour* tape.

Allow time for a Dynamo Special or two. Do not get stuck in a musical rut. Watch for artistic and dramatic talents which can be developed during this time.

Getting the Message Across (6 minutes)

To define *communication* give this simple object lesson, using two slices of bread, peanut butter, and jelly.

A rather complicated definition of *communication* is "the exchange of thoughts, messages, or information, as by speech, signals, or writing." It is simply "getting the message across."

Call a child to the front and give her a note asking her to do a simple task, such as, open a door. After she does the task, continue.

She got the message. What are some other ways I could have communicated with her? Speech, telephone, sign language.

How did Indians communicate in pioneer days? Smoke signals.

What are some methods of communication used today? Radio, television, computer, newspaper, mail, telephone, FAX.

One way many visually-impaired people communicate is with braille—tiny raised bumps that they feel or "read" with their fingers. Pass the braille messages around and let the children feel. **This is how you spell "Jesus" in braille.**

Deaf people use sign language to communicate with other people. What is communicating with Jesus called? Prayer.

Communication is two-way. It is not just talking or listening.

I am going to make a "communication sandwich." Spread peanut butter on a slice of bread. **Peanut butter is like talking. It is good by itself, but to make this sandwich complete, we need something else—jelly!** Spread jelly on another slice. **The jelly is like listening.**

God likes to talk to us, too! If we do all the talking, we won't hear what He has to say. Put the sandwich together.

What are some ways God speaks to us? He may speak to you in a voice you can hear. But most likely He will speak to your heart. You will have this feeling inside you that God wants you to do or not do a certain thing—or that He loves you and forgives you. He also speaks to us through His Word, the Bible. That's why we like to memorize Scriptures. It is God's message to us, and we need to get the message.

Have the children repeat the *POWer line* after you several times. **Jesus is always with us. We can talk to Him any time.**

Lift Up Holy Hands (5 minutes)

Take prayer requests and lead the children in a congregational prayer. Close with praise and thanksgiving.

After you have talked to God, lead the children in this "listening exercise." Ask them to sit quietly with their heads bowed, eyes closed, and hands folded in their laps. Explain that to hear God's voice, we must get our minds on Him and think, "What do You want to tell me, Jesus? I'm listening." Allow fifteen or twenty seconds of absolute silence. Then end prayer time with "Amen."

Be sure the children understand that if they did not hear the Lord speak to them, they should not be alarmed. They should simply make a practice of listening each time they pray. When the Lord needs to speak to their hearts, He will. Until then, He is speaking to them through His Word as it is taught and preached and studied.

Pretzel Prayers (4 minutes)

Many years ago the pastor of a church reminded the children in his church to pray by giving them a "little gift," a "pretiola." This was a biscuit shaped like a pair of hands clasped in prayer. You know these little twists by the name "pretzel" now. Show one. **Notice how they look like little hands folded in prayer?**

Special

A Round of Applause to the Deaf Ministry

Surely the hands of people involved in the deaf ministry could be called "joyful hands."

If your church has a deaf ministry, arrange an interview with someone involved in it. Questions could include:

■ What got you interested in this ministry?

■ What kind of training have you had?

■ What is the hardest part of signing?

■ What is the most rewarding aspect of your ministry?

Let the children take part in the interview.

This could be the beginning of a "junior" deaf ministry.

Is there a child present who has been sick? Wearing the kid's glove for this *POWer hour* would be a day brightener for him.

Did you divide into teams for the offering? If so, give the winning team their awards as they leave.
Start anew with Unit Two.

Ask helpers to give each child a pretzel. **Every time you see a pretzel, let it remind you to pray—or communicate with God. Remember, that's talking and listening!**

When can we pray? Any time. **Where can we pray?** Anywhere.

What is the *POWer line*? **Jesus is always with us. We can talk to Him any time.**

From Our Hands to Yours (2 minutes)

As a lively chorus is played, let the children march around and give their offering. Keep them posted on the total.

POWer of the Word

From Hand to Heart (5 minutes)

Teach the children Mark 12:29-30 in sign language. If no one is available who does signing, make up motions to portray the words.

Example: **Hear** (point to ear) **o** (make o with thumb and forefinger) **Israel,** (arms out, palms up. What does this have to do with Israel? Nothing, but it is a memory key the children will understand.) **the Lord** (point up) **our** (sweeping motion of arm) **God** (wave hand toward heaven) **is one** (one finger up) **Lord** (point up).

Ask for volunteers who have memorized this passage to come to the front and recite it, using the microphone. Give each participant a round of applause as he adds his name to the Recited Memory Passage jar.

Worship Chorus (2 minutes)

Sing a worship chorus to prepare their hearts for the Word of the Lord.

ILLUSTRATED SERMON

This story is not meant to be read, but used as a guide. Read it until you are familiar with the actions and emotions. Then tell it in your words with the anointing of the Holy Ghost.

Disciples on the Road to Emmaus (10 minutes)

Our Bible story comes from the Book of Luke. Is Luke in the Old or New Testament? When you find Luke in your Bible, jump to your feet. When several are standing, continue.

Luke is one of the books of the Bible, called the Gospels, which tells the story of Jesus' life on earth. It starts with the story of His birth and ends with His ascension into heaven. The story I am going to tell you happened after Jesus was crucified, so will it be near the beginning or the end of the book? The end. **Turn to chapter 24.** After most of the children have found it, congratulate them. Ask them to be seated and close their Bibles.

We communicate in more ways than just with spoken words. One way we communicate is called "body language." Ask the children what your body language is saying in each of these positions. (1) Cross your arms and slump down in your chair. (2) Sit down beside someone and turn your back to them. (3) Sit beside someone else and lean toward them. **Sometimes our body language speaks louder than our words.**

I am going to tell you the story with spoken words, and I want you to tell it with body language. Let's practice.

You are very sad. How do you look? Let children show you. If they do not know how to respond, show them a sad face and slumped shoulders.

You are surprised. What do you do? Mouth drops open. Eyes get big. Shoulders jerk.

You are excited. What do you do? Mouth forms "O." You jump up and down and clap your hands.

From time to time as I tell this story, I will stop and ask you to show me how the people in the story are feeling. Ready?

Two followers of Jesus were on their way home to Emmaus. It had been a long, hard weekend. Their best friend, Jesus, had been crucified. *How did these men look?*

Just before they left Jerusalem, they had heard some strange stories. Some of the women who followed Jesus had told them that they had gone to the tomb and Jesus was not there. Instead they had seen angels who had said that Jesus had risen from the dead.

More of their friends had gone to check out the women's story, and they, too, said the tomb was empty! Jesus was gone!

Now these two men on their way home to Emmaus were puzzled. They knew Jesus had died. They knew He had been buried. They wanted to believe He had risen from the dead, but that was impossible. Wasn't it? They were very, very puzzled. *How did they look?*

As they walked along and talked about the strange things that had happened, a stranger came near and joined them. They did not recognize Him, but the stranger was Jesus.

Jesus looked at their sad faces and slumped shoulders. "What are you talking about?" He asked. "Why are you so sad?"

They looked at Jesus in surprise. "Are you a stranger around here? Don't you know what has happened in the city?" *How did they look?*

"What things are you talking about?" Jesus asked.

So they began to tell Him all about how Jesus had been crucified and how the women and other disciples had said He had risen.

Jesus looked at them and shook His head. "Don't you understand what has happened? Christ had to suffer these things." And then He began to teach them.

The men were amazed. What Jesus was telling them was so interesting. *How did they look?*

They were so engrossed in what Jesus was saying, they could hardly believe it when they reached home. Jesus bid them "good day" and started down the road.

"Oh, sir," they said, "don't leave. Tell us more. It's getting dark. Come in and spend the night."

So Jesus went in with them. As they sat down to eat the evening meal, He gave thanks. As He passed the bread to the men, suddenly they recognized Him. They had been walking and talking with Jesus and didn't even know it! *How did they look now?*

Before they could say a word, Jesus was gone! Just like that, He vanished! *How did they look?*

"I knew it! I knew there was something different about Him! What He said was so powerful, my heart just burned in me as I listened to Him," one said.

"Quick!" the other disciple probably urged. "We've got to go back to the city and find the others. We must tell them that the Lord is risen indeed!" *How do you think they looked as they raced back to the city?*

What an exciting story! These men went from very sad to ecstatic in just a short time. And what made the difference? A little talk with Jesus.

Invitation and Prayer (5-? minutes)

Musician plays, "Let's Have a Little Talk with Jesus."

When we are sad, disappointed, or troubled, we can talk to Jesus, too. You do not have to be in church to talk to Him, although that is a good place to do it. Jesus is always with us. We can talk to Him anytime. You can talk to Him when you are alone or when you are in a crowd. You can talk to Him aloud or you can "think" a prayer.

If you have never repented of your sins and received the Holy Ghost, now is the time to talk to Jesus. He is listening, waiting for you to communicate with Him.

Encourage everyone to kneel at their seats and have a little talk with Jesus. Handymen and handmaidens should be sensitive to the Spirit and pray with the children as they feel led.

Review

Play Did You Get the Message?

Tell one thing you learned this *POWer hour*. Toss a small, soft ball to a child. That child must quickly tell something he learned and toss the ball to another child. Keep the ball moving.

Or play Pass the Question.

Write review questions on slips of paper, fold, and place in a basket. As the music plays, the basket is passed around. When the music stops, the child holding the basket draws a question. He then chooses someone to answer the question. If the question is answered correctly, it is thrown out. If it is not, it is returned to the basket, and the music begins again.

Have the Hands-Full Jar drawings, including the grand prize drawing. Throw out the hand prints which have accumulated and start fresh next *POWer hour*. Give each child a *POWer house* paper as they leave. Remind the preschoolers that there is a letter on their paper for their parents.

Unit Two
Relationships

Unit Aim: To encourage children to reach out to others.

Memory Passage: Mark 12:31

Attendance Chart

This unit will need some continuing preparation. The suggested attendance chart calls for a hand print for each child at each *kids POWer hour*. If you have thirty children, you will use one hundred fifty hand prints in the next five weeks.

As the children enter, they sign their name and the date on a hand print. The hand prints are then used to spell the caption: Helping Hands. Or the caption may be made in advance and the children sign the prints on the board—or make new ones to form the border. Children may be given new hand prints each *POWer hour* or add the date to the original one.

Note to the Teacher

The times given in this unit are approximate. If an activity meets a need in your group or if the children are extremely involved and interested, spend more time doing it. Always remember you are there to teach your kids, not a lesson plan.

Alternate Suggestion for Attendance Chart

Have one large hand premade, and let each child either write their name on the hand or on a self-stick label and put that on the hand.

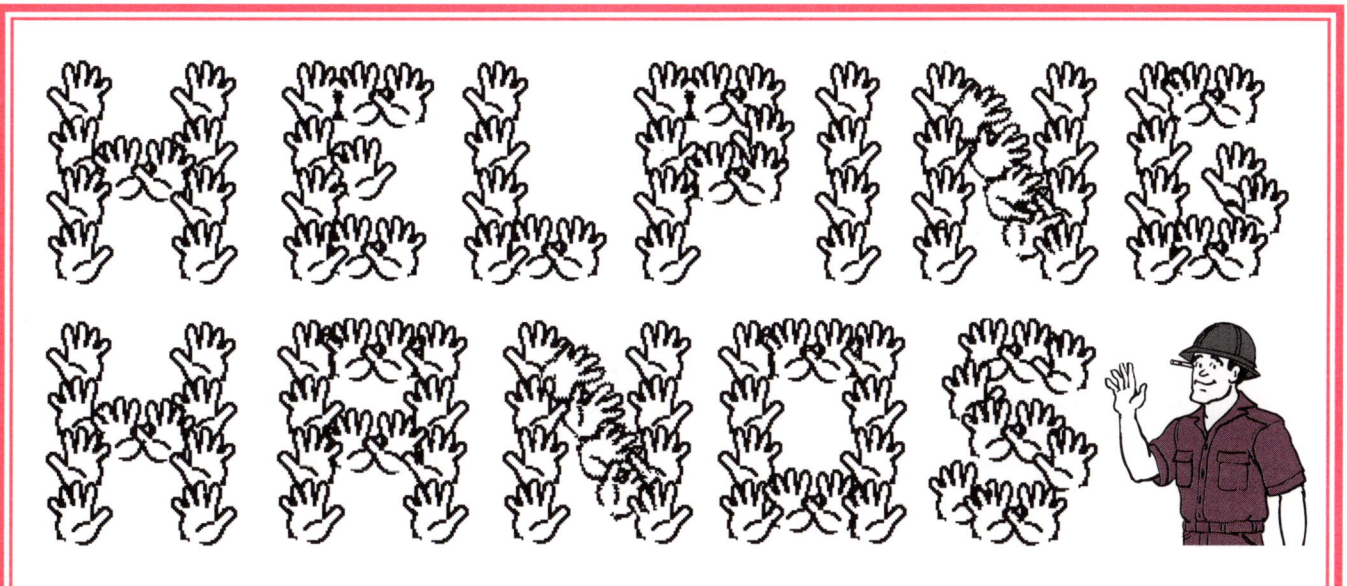

J = Jesus First
O = Others Second
Y = You Last

Unit Two
Relationships

Unit Aim: To encourage children to reach out to others.

Memory Passage: Mark 12:31

Jesus' Right Hands

Scripture Text: Mark 12:29-34; Matthew 25:31-46

 True joy comes when we put Jesus and others before self.

Schedule
Date: _____
I. POWer of Worship (30-35 minutes)
  A. Welcome (8 minutes)
    • Hands-Full Jars and Attendance Chart
    • Help Me Remember
    • Announcements
    • Right Hand Man
  B. Lift Up Holy Hands (4 minutes)
  C. Sing unto the Lord (6 minutes)
    • Praise Choruses
    • Dynamo Specials
  D. Stand Up for Jesus (3 minutes)
  E. From Our Hands to Yours (5 minutes)
  F. POWer line Unscramble (4 minutes)
  G. Handcuffed (4 minutes)
II. POWer of the Word (25-30 minutes)
  A. From Hand to Heart (5 minutes)
  B. Worship Chorus (3 minutes)
  C. Handy Dan Needs Help (4 minutes)
  D. Illustrated Sermon (8 minutes)
    • Jesus' Right Hands
  E. Invitation and Prayer (5-? minutes)
  F. Review

 **Shop Talk**

✓ Handy Dan needs a sling for his right arm, two sandwiches, sandwich bags, and his toolbox, along with a copy of the script, "Handy Dan Needs Help."
✓ As the children enter, choose five to help with the Illustrated Sermon. They will come to the front when called for, each carrying one of the following: (1) clothes, (2) a cup of water, (3) something to eat, (4) a pillow and blanket, and (5) tracts and a Bible.
✓ Arrange for the director of a department in your church (preferably the department to which your current offering is going) to come to tell the children how offerings help his department. Give him a time limit.
✓ Cut out of bright colored paper, large letters: J-O-Y.
✓ Write each word of the POWer line on an index card. Make one set for each four to six children.
✓ Write each word of Mark 12:31 on a flashcard large enough to be seen by every child.
✓ Make large tic-tac-toe game cards (5 X's and 5 O's) to hang around the players' necks. Lay out a gameboard on the floor with masking tape.
✓ Decide on the criteria for wearing the kid's glove. How about looking for helping hands? Did anyone help a neighbor or sick friend?
✓ Make a supply of hand prints for the Hands-Full Jars and attendance chart.

POWer of Worship

On Hand

- ❏ *kids POWer hour* tape
- ❏ tape player
- ❏ *POWer house* papers
- ❏ construction paper hand prints
- ❏ Hands-Full Jars
- ❏ joyful gloves and kid's glove
- ❏ bright colored art paper
- ❏ index cards
- ❏ clothes
- ❏ cup of water
- ❏ food
- ❏ pillow and blanket
- ❏ tracts and Bible
- ❏ strips of cloth, old ties, or toy handcuffs
- ❏ ball
- ❏ song book
- ❏ paper and pencil
- ❏ two sandwiches
- ❏ sandwich bags
- ❏ toolbox
- ❏ review notebook
- ❏ timer
- ❏ tic-tac-toe game cards of posterboard or art paper
- ❏ yarn or string
- ❏ masking tape

Welcome (8 minutes)

Handymen and handmaidens, wearing joyful gloves, greet each child by name or have each child introduce his guest. The Handy Helpers help each child write his name and date on a hand print and add them to the "Helping Hands" bulletin board.

Continue the Hands-Full Jars activity. Remove the Recited Memory Passage jar for this *POWer hour*.

Handy Dan is again on hand to visit with the children and "fix" things. If a child comes to *kids POWer hour* with his "smiler" broken, Dan may need to tell silly riddles or jokes. Many children come from unhappy homes, and they need to know that God's house is a happy place. It's okay to laugh at church.

Variety is the spice of life and of *kids POWer hour*. Keep the children guessing. Start this *POWer hour* with a review game, "Help Me Remember."

Say, "Susan, please help me remember . . . " and ask a question from last week, such as, "Who was walking on the road to Emmaus?" Susan remembers the fact, and then she asks another child, "Johnny, please help me remember. . . ." Johnny will supply Susan's answer and ask another child to help him remember a specific fact. Allow only a few minutes for this activity. If a child stalls on asking a question, supply one from your review notebook.

Make announcements, welcome guests, and acknowledge birthdays.

Define "right hand man" by asking one of the handymen or handmaidens (or one of the children) to bring you something from the back of the room. Refer to this person as your "right-hand man," whether boy or girl. Stress the importance of "right hands." Point out that for left-handed children their left hand is the "right hand" for doing most of their work.

Our lesson title is "Jesus' Right Hands." We are going to learn how we can be Jesus' right-hand men.

The Handy Helpers should be giving joyful handshakes from time to time, rewarding children for good behavior and participation.

Lift Up Holy Hands (4 minutes)

Have the children tell of someone or something that needs help. Pray for puppies and kittens with the same sincerity that you pray for someone with cancer.

Have the children pick one request that they will pray for every day this week. Explain that when we pray, we are God's right-hand men.

Sing unto the Lord (6 minutes)

Use the *kids POWer hour* tape to review the memory passage by singing, "Two Great Commandments." Learn the second verse of the theme song, "My J-O-Yful Hands."

"You're My Brother, You're My Sister, So Take Me by the Hand"

Dynamo Specials

Tell the children that this *POWer hour's* Dynamo Specials are going to be a bit different. Call for volunteers to do various things, such as pick up song books, bring the Helping Hands attendance poster to the front, possibly even pick up trash. After each job, let the entire congregation know that *(name)* has had a special helping part in the service. Give each participant a round of applause.

Stand Up for Jesus (3 minutes)

Have a sentence testimony service, asking the children to finish this sentence. **"I can help _____ by _____."** Set the timer and stop when the timer goes off, even if a child is in the middle of a sentence.

From Our Hands to Yours (5 minutes)

Have a director of one of your church's departments tell how giving helps that particular department. Have them emphasize the fact that each time a child gives, a specific need is met. For example, if the outreach director talks to your group, have him bring a tract and tell the children that for each specific amount of money, a certain number of tracts can be bought to give to those that do not know Christ.

If you have set up a display of tracts in foreign languages as suggested on page 8, refer to them at this time. Foreign missionaries tell of many times when one tract has lead to the salvation of an entire village.

POWer line Unscrambled (4 minutes)

Divide into groups of four to six. Give each group a set of the *POWer line* word cards. See which group can put the *POWer line* in the proper order first. One rule: no talking! When they finish, they should quietly raise their hands until the director acknowledges that they have been seen. Call for the teams to read their *POWer line* in the order they finished. If the children need a clue to get started, tell them that the first word of the *POWer line* starts with a capital and it is not "Jesus." Also tell them the last word.

True joy comes when we put Jesus and others before self.

Handcuffed (4 minutes)

Ask for volunteers. Choose various ages. Use strips of cloth, old ties, or toy handcuffs to tie their hands behind their backs—very lightly as they will be in this position for several minutes. Ask them to do various activities using their hands. Examples: catch a ball, write their name, shake hands with a visitor.

When they are unable to do it, comment on the importance of our hands. Explain that you will need the volunteers again later and have them sit down, hands still tied.

POWer of the Word

From Hand to Heart (5 minutes)

Use this time to define both the words and the meaning of Mark 12:31.
Have the students find the Scripture in the Bible. Pair non-readers with older students.

> Children are basically very self-centered. The majority have a whole world that revolves around them—and they enjoy it. As spiritual leaders, part of our job is to train them to be sensitive to the needs of others.

Write each word on an index card. Put the words on a board or the wall in phrases. Example: *"And the second is like, namely this."* Discuss each phrase briefly.

Then read the entire verse from the Bible.

Worship Chorus (3 minutes)

Lead the children in a worship chorus to prepare their hearts for the Word of the Lord.

Handy Dan Needs Help (4 minutes)

Handy Dan comes to the front with his right arm in a sling, hair messed up, and holding two sandwiches, which he is trying to stuff into sandwich bags.

DAN: **Oh boy! Oh boy. Oh boy. I don't know what I'm going to do. I've got to go to work and I can't get my lunch packed.** Continues muttering to himself and unsuccessfully trying to get the sandwiches into the bags.

DIRECTOR: **Hi, Dan. What is going on? You look like you are in trouble.**

DAN: **Oh, hello, Sister** *(director)*. **You would not believe what happened to me. Last week I broke my arm when I fell off a roof. Then this morning I didn't hear my alarm clock and I overslept. Now, I need to be at work and I can't pack my lunch, and I'm not ready for work, and I'm going to go crazy! I didn't realize how much I need my right arm.**

DIRECTOR: **Poor Dan. You really do have a problem. I'll tell you what. I may be able to help. I'll pack your lunch while you get your hair combed and your tools together.**

DAN: **Oh, would you? That would be wonderful. Thank you.**

DAN EXITS and combs hair while the teacher puts the sandwiches in bags.
DAN ENTERS ready for work, toolbox in hand.

DIRECTOR: **There you are, Dan. One lunch ready to go.**

DAN: **Oh, thanks. I don't know what I would have done without you.**

DAN EXITS, whistling. Director watches him, then looks thoughtful.

DIRECTOR: **I'm glad I could help Dan. He really needed it. When I helped him, something else happened—inside me. It made me feel good way down in my heart to help him. Jesus talked about helping others. Let's read it in the Bible.**

PERMISSION TO COPY SCRIPT

ILLUSTRATED SERMON

Jesus' Right Hands (8 minutes)

Have the children turn to Matthew 25 with the older children helping the younger.

I have a listening assignment for you. As I read verses 31-46, follow along in your Bible and count every time I read "right hand." (two times)

Just as the children could not perform assigned tasks with their hands tied behind their backs, Jesus needs us to do His work. One of the advantages to being used by God is that it brings us joy.

To emphasize this point, show the letters J-O-Y and then scramble them. Try to spell "joy" ojy, yoj, oyj, yjo, jyo. **"Joy" cannot be spelled any way but J-O-Y.**

There is also no way we can live a successful Christian life unless we put Jesus first, Others second, and You third.

Jesus instructed us that each time we feed the hungry (child brings out the food), **give a drink to the thirsty** (child brings out the glass of water), **help the homeless** (child brings out the pillow and blanket), **share our clothes** (child brings out clothing), **or visit those who are in prison or cannot come to church** (child brings out tract and Bible), **we are acting as Jesus' hands.**

When we use our hands to help Jesus, we feel good deep down inside. It makes us smile and sing. It makes us laugh and laugh. To be used as the hands of Jesus is the highest privilege a Christian can experience.

Have your tied up students come back to the front. Ask them if they could do the assigned task. Then choose a helper for each one. The helper and the child work together to do the task.

We can help no matter what our age. Have the students tell some ways they could help at home, at school, at church, etc. Emphasize that when we help, we become God's hands because we are following the second most important commandment.

Invitation and Prayer (5-? minutes)

Have the students who would like to be God's hands this next week come to the front. Lead in prayer reminding each to look for ways that they can be God's hands.

If there are students who do not have the Holy Ghost, ask them if they would like to have this Pentecostal experience. Then they, too, can be a part of the body of Christ and be used as God's hands.

Review

Divide into two groups, the X's and the O's, for a giant tic-tac-toe game. Ask a review question to the first player. If he answers correctly, hang a game card around his neck and instruct him to stand in the square of his choosing on the game board. Next question goes to the opposing team. Continue until there are three team members in a row. Then "erase" the board and start over.

Have the Hands-Full Jar drawing. Remind each that they can be a winner next *kids POWer hour*.

Use the back of the *POWer house* to send home announcements of church services and activities, or write a note affirming the child. Give each child a *POWer house* paper as he leaves.

Unit Two
Relationships

Unit Aim: To encourage children to reach out to others.

Memory Passage: Mark 12:31

Hands Reaching Out

Scripture Text: Jeremiah 38:1-13

 We should reach out to others, no matter what their race.

J = Jesus First
O = Others Second
Y = You Last

 **Shop Talk**

✓ If you do not have the Dynamo kid puppets, use the art in the back of this manual to make sack puppets: a white girl, a black boy, a Hispanic girl, and an Oriental boy. Make five copies of the script and have a practice session.

✓ Make a supply of hand print cutouts for the Hands-Full Jars, the review game, and the attendance chart. Write a review question on enough hands so there is one for each chair. Tape each to the bottom of a chair with the question face down.

✓ Handy Dan needs two short pieces of 2 x 4's, a hammer, a nail apron, and several different sizes of nails, a dozen or so of each.

✓ If there is someone from another culture available, invite the person to *kids POWer hour* to share some of the things he or she found strange when first coming to America. Limit him to about five minutes. If he is reluctant to speak publicly, ask him to share these things with you so you can relate them to the children.

✓ Write each word of Mark 12:31 on an index card. Make one set for each four to six children.

✓ Display an attractive arrangement of real or silk flowers on a table in front of the room.

✓ Add review questions based on this *POWer hour's* material to your notebook.

✓ Make copies of the *POWer house* papers.

Schedule

Date: _____

I. POWer of Worship (30-35 minutes)
  A. Welcome (8 minutes)
    • Kids Are Like Flowers
    • Identify the Pattern
    • Announcements
  B. Sing unto the Lord (6 minutes)
    • Praise Choruses
    • Dynamo Specials
  C. Another Culture (5 minutes)
    • A Guest Speaker
  D. Lift Up Holy Hands (3 minutes)
    • Prayer for Missionaries
  E. Stand Up for Jesus (4 minutes)
  F. From Our Hands to Yours (3 minutes)
  G. A Lesson from the Nail Apron (4 minutes)
II. POWer of the Word (20-25 minutes)
  A. From Hand to Heart (6 minutes)
    • Mark 12:31
  B. Worship Chorus (2 minutes)
  C. Puppet Skit (5 minutes)
    • Needed: A Friend
  D. Illustrated Sermon (10 minutes)
    • Jeremiah's Friend
  E. Invitation and Prayer (5-? minutes)
  F. Review
    • Turn Around

On Hand

- ❏ *kids POWer hour* tape
- ❏ tape player
- ❏ hand print cutouts (for Hands-Full Jars and attendance chart)
- ❏ Hands-full jars
- ❏ joyful gloves and kid's gloves
- ❏ small prizes
- ❏ puppets of Dynamo kids (sack puppets will do)
- ❏ tacks or Plastic-tak
- ❏ variety of nails, such as, roofing, colored paneling, 16 penny, tacks
- ❏ nail apron
- ❏ two short pieces of 2 x 4's
- ❏ hammer
- ❏ black construction paper
- ❏ scissors
- ❏ old rope
- ❏ rags
- ❏ silk or live floral arrangement
- ❏ index cards
- ❏ *POWer house* papers

> Children are wonderful observers. They are very quick to notice differences. They are also quick to assimilate parental prejudices. In training leaders, we need to (1) examine our lives for any prejudices we might have and pray until we no longer have them, and (2) teach our children that different is not necessarily bad.

POWer of Worship

Welcome (8 minutes)

Once again the handymen and handmaidens greet the children with joyful handshakes and help them with the Hands-Full Jars activity. For the attendance chart, have the children write their names and the date on a hand print. If they have helped someone during the past week, ask them to draw a star on the palm. Tack the hand print to the Helping Hands bulletin board.

Handy Dan should make a point of watching for children who are shunned by the other children. He should pray for wisdom to be a peacemaker and help the children build friendships with those who are "different."

Give the crowd control signal and lead in a brief prayer.

As some of the smaller children may not understand "race," define the term.

A simple object lesson which all ages can grasp is a bouquet of flowers. Refer to the arrangement you have on display. In the bouquet are flowers of different colors and kinds, but all beautiful. God has beautified His creation with children of all colors, sizes, and shapes.

Ask the children to repeat the *POWer line* several times. **We should reach out to others, no matter what their race.**

Involve the children in an Identify the Pattern exercise.

The purpose of this activity is to show that everyone has common and differing characteristics.

Tell the children that you are going to call some to the front and you want them to stand in the exact order in which they are called. Inform the rest of the group that you are going to make a pattern with the children in front and their job is to guess what that pattern is. Tell them that it might be something that they are wearing or something about their body. It could be anything. As soon as they think that they know what the pattern is, they should raise their hand. Keep repeating the pattern until the children identify it.

Call the children by name to form a specific pattern—example: boy, girl, boy, girl; or brown hair, blond hair; or tied shoes, non-tied shoes. Emphasize that Jimmy, Johnny, and Sam are alike in some ways, but different in others. Let the children know that one is not better than the other, just different. Each is loved by God.

Alternate Approach: Use the same emphasis only call out a characteristic such as wearing tennis shoes and have all the children who are wearing tennis shoes stand. Spend a few minutes finding out what other kinds of shoes are being worn. Again, emphasize there are no better or worse—only different.

Make announcements, acknowledge birthdays, and welcome guests.

Sing unto the Lord (6 minutes)

"Why Don't You Lift Up Your Hands and Praise the Lord?"
"My J-O-Yful Hands"
"J-O-Y-F-U-L H-A-N-D-S"
"Reach Out and Touch the Lord"

For the Dynamo specials ask for volunteers to tell about friends that are of a different race.

Another Culture (5 minutes)

Introduce the person from another culture to the children (or share what you learned from him). Explain that we often think of other cultures as "strange," but we do not often stop to realize that we are just as different to them as they are to us.

Lift Up Holy Hands (3 minutes)

Use this prayer time to emphasize prayer for the missionaries. Missionaries must learn to adapt to various cultures before they can be successful in the work God has called them. They depend on the prayers of the church at home.

Stand Up for Jesus (4 minutes)

Pick hands that have been marked with a star from the Helping Hands bulletin board. Have them tell in a few sentences how they helped someone during the last week.

Alternate Approach: Have a child tell how a friend helped him.

From Our Hands to Yours (3 minutes)

Remind children of the offering project. Ask a handyman or handmaiden to lead in prayer, asking God's blessings upon the project.

Take the offering this *POWer hour* by handing your offering to the first child on the first row. That child adds his offering and hands it to the next child, and so on. If you have a large group, have the ushers pick up the money at the end of the row. For a small group, you may be able to let the offering pass from hand to hand until it is taken. Children will enjoy watching and feeling it grow. Do not worry about anyone pocketing some. Everyone will be watching too closely.

A Lesson from the Nail Apron (4 minutes)

Handy Dan starts pounding at his work bench. He explains that he is trying to nail the 2 x 4's together. He pulls from his nail apron different nails which will not do the job, such as, a paneling nail, a tack, a roofing nail, saving the right nail for last. He emphasizes that every nail is not made to hold 2 x 4's together, but every nail has a purpose. He explains each nail's use. He points out that nails, like people, come in different colors and sizes, but all are important.

POWer of the Word

From Hand to Heart (6 minutes)

Can anyone quote Mark 12:29-30 from last unit? If so, give them a "joyful" handshake. If only one can quote it, give him the kid's glove to wear.

Sing, "Two Great Commandments," using the *kids POWer hour* tape.

Divide the class into groups of four to six, mixing ages. Give each group a set of memory verse cards.

Have the children sit on the floor and arrange the cards in correct order. When a group is finished, they stand and wait quietly. When all groups are finished or time is called, everyone reads the Scripture together. Collect the cards for next week.

Worship Chorus (2 minutes)

Lead the children in a worship chorus to quiet their spirits and prepare them to listen to the Word.

Puppet Skit (5 minutes)

Use the Dynamo kids to present the puppet skit on page 47.

• ▶

Have you ever had someone make fun of you? How did it make you feel? It hurts my heart when I hear one child say to another, "I don't like you. I don't want to be your friend." I wonder if it hurts God's heart, too. We are all His children, and it must make Him feel sad when His children do not love one another.

Refer back to the flower arrangement. Discuss the fact that God made each of us unique and special and that He loves us. But sometimes people do not understand.

ILLUSTRATED SERMON

Jeremiah's Friend (10 minutes)

We find our Bible story in the Book of Jeremiah. **To find Jeremiah, open your Bible near the middle. Now flip slowly forward toward the New Testament until you find Jeremiah.** Spell it to help younger children. **Turn to chapter 38. The story I am going to tell you is found in the first thirteen verses of that chapter. Now you can close your Bibles.**

God gave Jeremiah a hard job. He had to preach judgment to his backslidden friends. It was not a popular message and it made Jeremiah lots of enemies. Jeremiah is called "the weeping prophet" because he cried so much.

For many, many generations the children of Judah had worshiped idols. Jeremiah pled with them to repent, but the people laughed at him. Eventually, God allowed King Nebuchadnezzar to come with his army and surround the city of Jerusalem.

God gave Jeremiah a message for the people. "If you will surrender to the enemy," Jeremiah warned, "your lives will be spared. If you do not surrender, the enemy will defeat you. Many will die and others will be carried away as prisoners-of-war."

This message made the people very angry. They went to the king. "Jeremiah's a traitor," they said. "He is on the enemy's side. We need to shut him up."

The wimpy little king whined, "Do whatever you want to him. I can't do anything against you."

Fold a sheet of black construction paper and cut, following the pattern, as you teach.

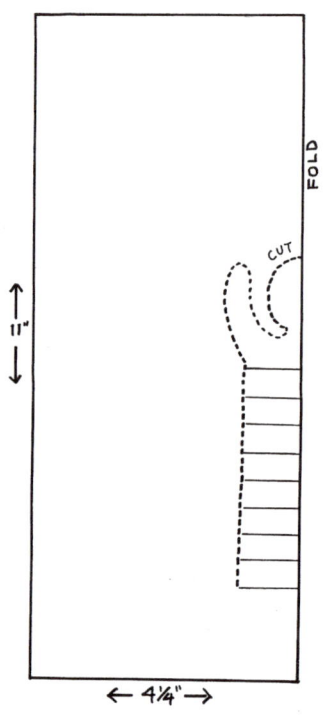
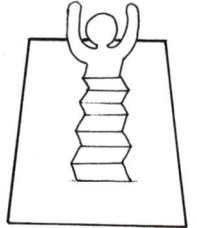

Needed: A Friend

ENTER ORIENTAL BOY with head down. Handy Dan stands outside the stage to converse with the puppets.

DAN: **Asa, you look way down. Is something wrong?**
ORIENTAL: Sniffs loudly. **Nah . . . well, not really . . . uhhh, well, kind of. . . .**
DAN: **What is it? Do you want to tell me?**
ORIENTAL: Shakes head no.
DAN: **Ahhh, come on. Usually when we are feeling down, it helps to talk about it.**
ORIENTAL: Sniffs again. **But . . . but it's hard to talk about it.**
DAN: **Just tell me what it is.** Pulls out hammer. **Old Handy Dan will have it fixed in no time. Tell me all about it.**
ORIENTAL: **It's . . . it's nothing you can fix. It's just that I brought a special Korean lunch, and some kids acted like I had done something really stupid.**

ENTER BLACK PUPPET.

BLACK: **Who acted like you did something stupid? What did you do? Was it stupid?**
DAN: **Asa didn't do anything stupid. In fact, his mother sent some of her Korean food to me one time. It wasn't stupid. It was good!** Rubs his stomach and licks his lips.
ORIENTAL: **Well, the kids didn't seem to think so. They thought it was yucky! They didn't think. . . .**

ENTER WHITE GIRL AND HISPANIC GIRL.

GIRLS: **Who didn't think?**
DAN: **You girls just gave the best answer I've heard to Asa's situation. People sometimes don't think before they talk.**
BLACK: **Asa brought a special Korean lunch to school and the kids made fun of it.**
HISPANIC: **My momma said that people sometimes get frightened if they don't understand something or something is new to them. Then they laugh because they don't know what else to do.**
ORIENTAL: **Do you think that's what happened?**
WHITE: **I do. Some people don't realize God made each of us special—so special that there will never be another one like us—no matter what color our skin is, what we eat, or where we live.**
BLACK: **Say, Asa. Do you have any of that lunch left?**
ORIENTAL: **Yes, I do.**
BLACK: **I think I should get a big taste and then I can tell everyone that they missed out on the bestest, scrumptious, wonderfulest lunch in the whole world. I'll be very glad to help you eat it.**

EXIT ALL, laughing.

PERMISSION TO COPY SCRIPT

Patterns on pages 126-127.

If you do not have puppets, keep these Dynamo kid sack puppets for future puppet scripts.

Line up top of face to folded edge of sak and glue in place.

Tuck lower half of face into crease of under-fold and glue.

So the people—people from Jeremiah's own country—took him and threw him in a dungeon—an old well. There was no water in the well, but there was lots and lots of mud. Fold on the solid lines so Jeremiah appears to sink into the mud. **Jeremiah sunk deeper and deeper into the mud. It seemed he would die.**

Then a man from the far country of Ethiopia, a servant in the king's palace, discovered what had happened. Ebedmelech was not even the same race as Jeremiah, but it upset him for a human to be treated as Jeremiah was being treated. He went to the king.

"Jeremiah is going to die if something is not done to save him," he told the king.

The king sighed. Why was everyone coming to him with their trouble? Didn't he have enough of his own?

"Then get some help and get him out of the dungeon," the king snapped.

Ebedmelech took ropes, old rags, and thirty men to help him. Thirty men to pull one man out of a pit? Jeremiah must have really been stuck in the mud! If you have a large group, line up thirty children along the rope.

On one end of the rope Ebedmelech tied old rags. He lowered them into the dungeon. "Put these under your arms so the rope won't burn you as we pull you out," he told Jeremiah.

Carefully Jeremiah obeyed. If possible, tie the end of the rope around the leg of a heavy table or object which can be moved without danger or damage. **When he was ready, Ebedmelech gave the order. "Pull. Gently now."** The children should pull as if pulling Jeremiah from the pit. **"Careful now. Don't hurt him. He's almost at the top. Here he comes. There! Jeremiah is out of the pit. Thank you. Thank you very much!"**

Don't you know that Jeremiah was glad that God had sent Ebedmelech to help? Ebedmelech was not prejudiced. He reached out to Jeremiah even though Jeremiah was a different color than he was and belonged to a different race.

What's the *POWer line*? We should reach out to others, no matter what their race.

Invitation and Prayer (5-? minutes)

End the service on an evangelistic note by comparing Ebedmelech, the Ethiopian, pulling Jeremiah out of the dungeon to God pulling us out of the pit of sin. He wants us to go to heaven where there will be no racial or cultural differences.

Review

Call for specific children, such as, eight-year-olds, to remove the questions from the bottom of their chairs. If they know the answer, they should remain standing. Go down the row letting them read their question and answer it. If they do not know the answer, they should give the question to the game leader. Once the question has been removed from a chair, the chair should be turned around facing the back wall. After the children answer or turn in their question, they sit down facing the back.

Call for another group, such as, everyone wearing red. These children remove their questions and go through the same procedure. Continue until all questions have been removed and chairs turned around. Then move to the back of the room and use the unanswered questions for a free-for-all quiz.

Have the Hands-Full Jar drawings.

Give each child a *POWer house* paper as he leaves.

Unit Two
Relationships

Unit Aim: To encourage children to reach out to others.

Memory Passage: Mark 12:31

Healing Hands

J=Jesus First
O=Others Second
Y=You Last

Scripture Text: Luke 10:25-37

 My neighbor is anyone who needs me.

 **Shop Talk**

✓ For the review game, place questions in balloons, blow up, and tie. Store in a garbage bag. (An alternate approach is also given for a review game at the end of this hour's material.)
✓ For the Illustrated Sermon draw faces on five giant balloons: (1) weary traveler, (2) proud priest, (3) busy, hurried Levite, (4) kind Samaritan, and (5) innkeeper. Cut the "feet" out of posterboard, sized to match the balloon. (See illustration in the margin on page 52.) The balloon puppets sit in front of the room as attention getters and are used to act out the lesson as the teacher tells the story. Choose four children to be the balloon puppeteers. A practice session will make the story move smoother.
✓ Make copies of the get acquainted game and the *POWer house* papers for each child.
✓ Get permission from your pastor, then invite one of the church elders to *kids POWer hour* to pray for the sick.
✓ Use one set of memory verse cards from last *kids POWer hour*. Attach a paper clip in the end of each card. Glue a magnet on the finger of two cloth gloves with tacky glue.
✓ On a computer make a banner of the *POWer line* and display in the front of the room. If you do not have a banner program, ask around. Someone in your church will have one or access to one.

Schedule
Date: _____
I. POWer of Worship (25-30 minutes)
  A. Welcome (8 minutes)
    • Let's Get Acquainted Game
    • Announcements
  B. Sing unto the Lord (6 minutes)
    • Praise Choruses
    • Dynamo Kids Choir
  C. Lift Up Holy Hands (5 minutes)
    • James 5:14-15
  D. Stand Up for Jesus (4 minutes)
  E. From Our Hands to Yours (3 minutes)
  F. A Lesson from the Toolbox (3 minutes)
II. POWer of the Word (25-30 minutes)
  A. From Hand to Heart (8 minutes)
    • Glove Detective
  B. Worship Chorus (2 minutes)
  C. Illustrated Sermon (8 minutes)
    • The Good Samaritan
  D. Invitation and Prayer (5-? minutes)
  E. Review
    • Balloon Burst

On Hand

- ❏ *kids POWer hour* tape
- ❏ tape player
- ❏ hand print cutouts (for Hands-full Jars and attendance chart)
- ❏ Hands-Full jars
- ❏ banner of the *POWer line*
- ❏ joyful gloves and kid's gloves
- ❏ small prizes
- ❏ copies of game, one per child
- ❏ pencils, one per child
- ❏ timer
- ❏ balloons—5 giant ones and numerous smaller ones
- ❏ posterboard (for balloon feet)
- ❏ band-aid can
- ❏ copies of script
- ❏ markers
- ❏ a pair of cloth gloves
- ❏ two short magnet strips
- ❏ tacky glue
- ❏ paper clips
- ❏ memory verse word cards
- ❏ hammer
- ❏ wooden object which can be destroyed
- ❏ band-aids

POWer of Worship

Welcome (8 minutes)

Handy Dan and the Handy Helpers welcome the children, giving away big smiles and joyful handshakes. Is there a child present who has been in an accident the past week? It does not have to have been life-threatening. A bicycle wreck resulting in a skinned elbow will do. Give that child the kid's glove to wear. Or the kid's glove could be worn by a child who brought his or her "neighbor" to *kids POWer hour*.

As the hands are added to the attendance chart, interlink the fingers.

Add names to hand prints and place in appropriate Hands-Full Jars.

Welcome the children and ask a couple of older ones to pass out the get acquainted game sheets and pencils. Preschoolers will need a helper.

Give the children a specified time to find others who fit these descriptions. A child's initials can only be on the paper in two places. However, the same child can sign for the same characteristic on any number of papers.

Alternate Approach: Play "Hot Seat." Call a student to the front to sit on the "hot seat." Let the rest of the group ask questions to determine his/her interests, likes, dislikes, family. Monitor the questions carefully for appropriateness.

Ask, "Who is my neighbor?" The children respond by reading the *POWer line*. **My neighbor is anyone who needs me.**

Getting to Know My Neighbor

Collector: _____

Find someone who matches each of these descriptions:

1. Someone who was not born in your city. _____
2. Someone who has a birthday in the same month as yours. _____
3. Someone who has a younger sister. _____
4. Someone who rides the bus to school. _____
5. Someone who lost a tooth in the last month. _____
6. Someone who took a trip last summer. _____
7. Someone who likes to work on computers. _____
8. Someone who helped their parents this week. _____
9. Someone whose middle name you do not know. _____
10. Someone who is your friend. _____

PERMISSION TO COPY SCRIPT

Sing unto the Lord (6 minutes)

"You're My Brother, You're My Sister"

For Dynamo Special have a traditional choir. Call all who would like to participate to the front to sing the theme song, "My J-O-Yful Hands."

Lift Up Holy Hands (5 minutes)

Read James 5:14-15: *"Is any sick among you? let him call for the elders of the church; and let them pray over him, anointing him with oil in the name of the Lord: And the prayer of faith shall save the sick, and the Lord shall raise him up; and if he have committed sins, they shall be forgiven him."*

Explain that in obedience to the Word of the Lord you have invited one of the church elders to *kids POWer hour* to pray for the sick. As the children's faith reaches out, miracles will happen! You can plan on it!

Stand Up for Jesus (4 minutes)

Have a variation of the popcorn testimony service. The teacher starts by saying, "I thank God for my neighbor, *(supply the name of a child sitting nearby)*, because. . . ." That person then stands and says, "I thank God for my neighbor, *(name)*, because. . . ." Continue the chain. See how many can testify in the allotted time.

From Our Hands to Yours (3 minutes)

Use a band-aid can as the offering plate. Discuss how the offering will be used to help heal those who are hurting.

A Lesson from the Toolbox (3 minutes)

Handy Dan starts hammering at his workbench, taking apart a wooden object, creating quite a disturbance. The director asks him what he is doing. Dan replies that he is tearing up something. The director says that he thought a hammer was designed to put things together. At this point Handy Dan gives the children an object lesson on a hammer, comparing it to our hands. We can use our hands to hurt or to heal.

POWer of the Word

From Hand to Heart (8 minutes)

Play glove detective. Lay the cards with a paper clip on one end, face down on the floor or a table.

Call two children to the front and give each a glove with the magnet on one finger. After each child uses the magnet to pick up a card, he gives the glove to the director and resumes his seat holding his card. Other children are called to repeat the activity. When all cards have been picked up, the children arrange themselves with cards displayed to form the correct reading of the verse.

Discuss what it means to love our neighbor as we love ourselves. **If you have two apples, one big and one little, which do you give to your neighbor and which do you keep for yourself? If you and your neighbor are tied for first place in a contest and there is only one prize, what do you do if you love your neighbor as yourself?**

Can anyone quote Mark 12:29-31? If so, let them add a hand to the Recited Memory Passage jar.

> Remember to give the crowd control clap at various intervals to keep the *POWer line* in the children's minds.

Worship Chorus (2 minutes)

Lead the children in a quiet worship chorus.

ILLUSTRATED SERMON

The Good Samaritan (8 minutes)

Sample shows balloons attached to and standing on feet. Pattern on page 124.

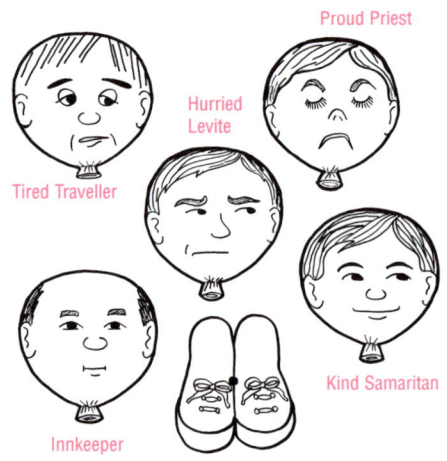

Our Bible story was once told by Jesus. Would we find it in the Old Testament or the New? Explain that the story of Jesus' life is found in the Gospels in the New Testament. **Turn to Luke 10. When you have found it, help your neighbor. Then stand.** When everyone is standing, ask them to be seated.

A lawyer came to Jesus and asked him, "Master, what do I have to do to be saved?"

Jesus answered, "You know the law. What does it say?"

The lawyer then quoted to Jesus our memory passage. Who will stand and quote Mark 12:29-31 for us? Or lead the children in quoting it together.

"Very good," Jesus answered.

But the lawyer was not content to stop there. He knew he had not been obeying it. He wanted to find an "out," so he asked, "Just who is my neighbor?"

To answer this question, Jesus told a parable, or a story. We call it, "The Parable of the Good Samaritan."

I've asked my balloon friends to help me tell this story. Call for four children to be the balloon puppeteers. The innkeeper does not need one. Puppeteers stand behind the balloons and move them as directed. Slip the Good Samaritan puppeteer some band-aids.

A certain man was traveling from Jerusalem to Jericho. Move the traveler slowly across the room. **This was a very dangerous journey. Robbers often hid among the rocks and attacked travelers.**

Oops! Watch out! Here comes a band of thieves! Oh dear, the poor man. They have stripped him and robbed him and beat him and left him for dead. Puppeteer removes the feet so the traveler lays on the floor. **Poor man. He lay beside the road, moaning in his half-conscious state.**

But wait. Here comes someone. The priest balloon moves slowly across the front, moving to one side to bypass the injured man. **It is a priest. Certainly this man of God will help. But what is he doing? Would you look at that? He is going around on the far side. Is this priest so busy he doesn't have time to help a dying man? What a shame!**

Here comes another man, a Levite. The Levite balloon moves slowly toward the injured man. **The Levites were the helpers who ministered in the Temple, much like music ministers, secretaries, and janitors do today. Like the priest, he was supposed to be a man of God.** Levite stops beside the man. **Oh, good, he is stopping. He must be deciding what he can do to help.** The Levite moves to far side and continues across the platform. **Oh, no, he is passing by on the far side just like the priest.**

I can't believe these people. Maybe they think the man is going to die anyway so why should they get their clean hands bloody. Maybe they think they are too busy to bother. Maybe they have their hands full of other things and won't put down their work to help. Whatever they think, this man is dying, and they are wrong not to help him.

Here comes another man. Samaritan moves slowly toward the injured man. **But I know he won't help because he is a Samaritan. The Samaritans and the Jews do not like each other. I can't see a Samaritan going out of his way to save the life of a Jew. Why, the Jews treat the Samaritans like dogs!**

Samaritan stops beside the injured man. **He's stopping, but I suppose he just wants to gloat.** Puppeteer puts band-aids on the injured man. **I can't believe it. Look! He is binding up the injured man's wounds.** The puppeteer picks up the injured man and carries him back to where the innkeeper stands.

The Samaritan picked up the man, put him on his donkey, and carried him to the inn (or hotel). There he took care of him until he had to leave. When he left, he gave the innkeeper some money and told him to care for the man. "If it costs you more than I have given you," the Good Samaritan said, "I will repay you when I come back."

Samaritan moves to the back of the room. Puppeteer puts the feet back on the traveler and stands him beside the innkeeper.

Then Jesus had a question for the lawyer, and I'll ask it to you. "Who was the injured man's neighbor?" The one who helped him.

Who is my neighbor? Children should read the *POWer line*. **My neighbor is anyone who needs me.**

The people that should have been the first to help did not. One had busy hands and one had non-involved hands—hands he did not want to get dirty. But a man who was looked down on by the Jews ignored prejudices and used his hands to heal.

Invitation and Prayer (5-? minutes)

Ask the children to put their hands in front of them and look at them. **How have you used your hands this week? Have you used them to fight? To hurt? To heal or make someone feel better?**

Ask the children to come to the altar to let Jesus touch their lives and make their hands healing hands. Remind them that this can only be done when we have the Holy Ghost.

Review

Pour out the review question balloons on the platform.

Call children up one at a time. Have them pick a balloon to pop. Ask them to read the question and then answer it or call on a neighbor to do so.

Alternate Approach: Cut the letters "n-e-i-g-h-b-o-r" out of construction paper. Post on the wall. Write one question on the back of each letter. Select a child to choose a letter and answer the question.

Have the Hands-Full Jars drawings.

Use the back of the *POWer house* paper to send a note home affirming the child, announce church activities and keep in touch with parents. Give each child a paper as he leaves.

For the practice session, use balls or other objects. Blow up the balloons just before *kids POWer hour*.

J = Jesus First
O = Others Second
Y = You Last

Unit Two
Relationships

Unit Aim: To encourage children to reach out to others.

Memory Passage: Mark 12:31

Helping Hands

Scripture Text: Mark 2:1-12

 We can help those who are disabled.

 **Shop Talk**

Schedule

Date: _____

I. POWer of Worship (25-30 minutes)
   A. Welcome (6 minutes)
      • Who Am I?
      • Announcements
   B. Sing unto the Lord (6 minutes)
      • Signing a Song
      • Dynamo Special
   C. Lift Up Holy Hands (4 minutes)
      • Prayer for the Disabled
   D. From Our Hands to Yours (3 minutes)
      • A Demonstration
   E. Stand Up for Jesus (4 minutes)
   F. *POWer line* Unscramble (3 minutes)
II. POWer of the Word (25-30 minutes)
   A. From Hand to Heart (6 minutes)
      • Relay Race: Mark 12:29
   B. Worship Chorus (2 minutes)
   C. A Lesson from the Work Bench (3 minutes)
   D. Illustrated Sermon (10 minutes)
      • Pantomime: Four Friends
   E. Invitation and Prayer (5-? minutes)
   F. Review

✓ To emphasize our need to help others who are disabled, play a game similar to "Who Am I?" Write the clues on index cards. Three identities are given here to get you started. Make up additional ones to fit the time slot. **(1) I look and dress just like you, except for my backpack. Some kids think I am a scuba diver because of the tank I carry everywhere I go. Who am I?** I am someone who has a lung disease. **(2) I sometimes have a special dog to help me. I read books with bumps. I am like Bartimaeus in the Bible. I sometimes use a white cane. Who am I?** I am a blind person. **(3) I am like everyone else until it is time to read. The letters just do not make sense to me. Sometimes I go to special classes. Who am I?** I am a child with a learning disability.

✓ Five children (preferably boys) are needed to pantomime the action as the director tells the Bible story. A practice session is helpful.

✓ Make copies of *POWer house* papers and gather supplies.

✓ Arrange for someone with a disability to speak to the children and give them tips on how to help the physically impaired. If possible, have someone who signs for the deaf come to *kids POWer hour* and sign as the children sing.

✓ Are you adding questions to your review notebook? How about information on new children, *e.g.*, addresses, phone numbers, birthdays.

✓ Write review questions on slips of paper and place in a pocket of a nail apron.

POWer of Worship

On Hand

- [ ] kids POWer hour tape
- [ ] tape player
- [ ] POWer house papers
- [ ] review notebook
- [ ] joyful gloves and kid's glove
- [ ] hand cutouts for Hands-full Jar and the attendance chart
- [ ] toolbox
- [ ] legal pad and pencil
- [ ] cloth for blindfold or old tie
- [ ] crutches (check at store or service organizations for loaners)
- [ ] blanket
- [ ] chalkboard and chalk or dry erase board and markers
- [ ] review questions
- [ ] nail apron
- [ ] small hammer

Welcome (6 minutes)

Handy Dan and the Handy Helpers stand at the door and greet the children with joyful handshakes as they enter. To emphasize the lesson aim Handy Dan has one foot wrapped and is on crutches. He should ask the children to help him do various jobs throughout the *POWer hour*.

Add hand cutouts to the Hands-Full Jars. After children have "signed in" on their hand print, arrange the prints in four-leaf clover formations on the attendance chart.

Give the crowd control clap.

Start by challenging the children to identify the "special" people in the "Who Am I?" game.

Welcome guests, acknowledge birthdays, and make announcements.

Sing unto the Lord (6 minutes)

Review signing the song the children learned in *POWer hour* 4.

Ask someone who signs for the deaf to come to *kids POWer hour* to sign as the children sing.

Allow time for at least one Dynamo Special.

Lift Up Holy Hands (4 minutes)

The apostle Paul had what he called "a thorn in the flesh." Some biblical scholars, people who spend lots of time studying the Bible, think it was a physical disability, perhaps poor eyesight. Paul prayed three times to be delivered, then accepted it as God's will.

God can heal any disease or affliction, but He does not always do it. Some people are given afflictions with which they must live all their lives.

Lead the children in praying for those with disabilities. Pray that God will bless these people and give the children wisdom to know how to help them.

From Our Hands to Yours (3 minutes)

Have junior ushers, one wearing a blindfold and the other on crutches, take up the offering.

Stand Up for Jesus (4 minutes)

I am special because. . . . Share a disability you have; perhaps you are short or overweight or wear glasses.

Encourage the children to do the same. If they are slow to respond, the Handy Helpers should fill in the gap by sharing their disabilities.

Emphasize that each one is special, no matter what his or her disability. Choose one of the children who testified (perhaps the first one) to wear the kid's glove.

POWer line Unscramble (3 minutes)

Write the scrambled *POWer line* on a board.

PLUG-IN

Have you ever been at a public place and watched as a child pointed to someone in a wheelchair and said, "What's wrong with that person?" It makes everyone somewhat uncomfortable.

Our purpose in this lesson is to help our children realize that everyone has characteristics that are the same and some that are different. Some can be seen while others are deeply hidden.

If we can make childen comfortable with differences and teach them good manners, we will make a vast difference in the lives of the disabled persons who enter our doors.

The teacher was a bit taken aback when her one of her juniors asked, "What's wrong with Terry?" The truth was Terry was mentally impaired.

"Yeah, what's wrong with him?" another asked.

The teacher noted that Terry was listening intently for her reply.

She took a deep breath and explained, "Terry's brain may have been injured at birth. You know, I have a disability. I am visually impaired and must wear glasses."

Catching the spirit of the teacher's intent, Kyle volunteered, "I have a bad knee."

One by one each junior discovered and shared how he or she was disabled.

The teacher relaxed, and Terry smiled. He wasn't so different, after all.

eW nca lpeh htose how era ableddis.

Work together to unscramble it. Or choose two boys and two girls and see who can unscramble it the quickest. Have the children read it together a couple of times.

POWer of the Word

From Hand to Heart (6 minutes)

Read together Mark 12:31. Place a chalkboard or markerboard at each end of the room. Divide into two teams and line up, facing opposite directions. The captain of each team stands beside the board to help preschoolers.

The first player runs to the board and writes the first word. He runs back, gives the chalk or marker to the next player, and goes to the back of the line. The next player runs to the board and adds the second word. Like Lot's wife, players are instructed "not to look back." Anyone caught peeking at the other team's board or telling a player the next word is out. Preschoolers whisper to the captain the next word which he writes on the board for them. Anyone who does not know the next word, drops out. A player can correct any mistakes made before him.

The first team to complete the verse correctly wins.

Let everyone who can quote the verse add a hand cutout to the Recited Memory Passage jar. Because of the time limit, you may have to take their word for it that they know the verse.

Worship Chorus (2 minutes)

Lead the children in a worship chorus to quieten their spirits and prepare their hearts for the Word of the Lord.

A Lesson from the Work Bench (3 minutes)

During the worship chorus, Handy Dan at the work bench takes his pencil from behind his ear and starts sketching on a legal pad.

DIRECTOR: **Handy Dan, what are you drawing?**
DAN: **Plans for a ramp into the church.**
DIRECTOR: **A ramp? What for? To slide down in the winter?**
DAN: **No. To help disabled people get in and out of the church. I didn't realize how important that was until I broke my foot. You'd be surprised how hard it is to get up and down stairs on crutches. And it is impossible in a wheelchair. And people with heart trouble often can't climb stairs.**
DIRECTOR: **It's nice of you to think of that.**
DAN: **I should have thought of it a long time ago. If I had, it would have been a lot easier for me to get into the church this morning.**
DIRECTOR: **We do want to make it easy for everyone to come to church to hear about Jesus. Our Bible story today is about that very thing.**
DAN: **Really? I didn't know anyone in the Bible built a ramp into the church.**
DIRECTOR: **They didn't build a ramp, but they did figure out a way to get a crippled man to Jesus.**

PERMISSION TO COPY SCRIPT

ILLUSTRATED SERMON

Four Friends (10 minutes)

As you tell the Bible story, five students pantomime the action.
Palsied man lays on a blanket in a corner in the back of the room.

When Jesus came to town, everyone knew it. Four men went running to their friend's house. "Jesus is in town," they told him excitedly. "He can heal you."

The poor man sighed. That would be wonderful, but how could he get to Jesus? He could not walk, and he could not call an ambulance because there were neither telephones nor ambulances in Bible days.

"Don't worry. We have come to take you to Jesus," said one of his friends. "We are going to carry you."

Each man picked up a corner of the sick man's bed and off they went to find Jesus. It was not hard. They knew all they had to do was find the biggest crowd in town and Jesus would be in the middle of it.

Sure enough, down the street they saw a house with people spilling out into the yard. "Jesus must be there," they agreed.

As they neared the house, they tried to work their way through the crowd. "Excuse us, please. We want to get our friend to Jesus." But everyone else wanted to get to Jesus, too. The men could not get to Him.

"It's hopeless," one may have said. "We'll never get through this mob."

"Let's put our load down and think about it," another could have suggested. So they lay their friend down gently. They thought and thought. They looked for an opening in the crowd. There was none.

One man snapped his fingers. "I know what we can do. Come with me." **The men picked up their friend. Away they went, around to the side of the house, up the outside stairway to the roof.** Boys can appear to be climbing the stairs by lifting their feet high. The ones in the front should hold the blanket higher than the ones in the back so the bed slants.

Houses in Bible days had flat roofs made of mud and sticks. When the men reached the top, they again lay down their friend. Quickly, they tore a hole in the roof. Imagine the poor people inside the house. What did they think when mud and sticks started falling on them?

As soon as the men had a hole big enough for their friend, they lowered him into the house, right in front of Jesus! You can be assured that the people got out of the way and made room for the bed coming through the roof!

Jesus looked up and smiled. He liked what He saw—four friends peering down into the room—friends with faith in their hearts and hands willing to help.

He looked at the sick man and said, "Your sins are forgiven." The friends may have felt a bit disappointed. They had brought their friend for healing. Instead Jesus was offering him salvation.

Some of the religious leaders frowned and thought, "Who does Jesus think He is to forgive sins? Only God can forgive sins."

Jesus knew exactly what they were thinking. He looked at them and asked, "Why are you thinking such things? Is it easier to forgive sins or heal the crippled?"

The religious leaders knew they could not do either one.

Jesus continued, "But so you will know that I have power to forgive sins, I'm going to show you something." He turned to the sick man, "Get up. Fold up your bed and go home."

The man who had not been able to walk, got up, picked up his bed, and went home!

His friends must have shouted and rejoiced as they followed him. "You should have been there," they told everyone. "We've never seen anything like it in our lives."

They had brought their friend for healing. Jesus had both forgiven and healed him.

Those who blocked the way had weak hands. The friends had helping hands. Jesus had healing hands. What kind of hands do you have?

We all need help in some way. A short person may need a ladder to stand on. A tall person may have to scrunch down in a small car. It is not a sign of weakness to need help, and it makes us feel very good to be the one to help someone else. What is the *POWer line*?

We can help those who are disabled.

Invitation and Prayer (5-? minutes)

Musician plays softly.

Even more than the man with palsy needed healing, he needed salvation. Having our sins forgiven is much more important than having a crippled limb healed, and blind eyes opened.

Jesus healed many people while He was on earth, but He did not come to earth just to heal the sick. He came to save the lost—those who did not know Him.

Briefly explain the plan of salvation. Ask those who need their sins forgiven to raise their hands. Then ask if they have a friend who will bring them to Jesus. If possible, have four children and/or helpers come to pray with each child.

Review

Have the children sit in a circle. As the music plays, in one direction pass a nail apron with review questions in one pocket. Pass a small hammer in the opposite direction. When the music stops, the child with the nail apron draws a question from the pocket and asks it to the child holding the hammer. Any time a child cannot answer a question, a "friend" can volunteer to answer for him. Answered questions are placed in a different pocket of the apron.

Have the Hands-Full Jars drawings.

Did any of the children get a response from the helping hand card in the last *POWer house*? If so, make time for them to share what their family did for the neighbor.

Give each child a *POWer house* paper as he leaves.

Unit Two
Relationships

Unit Aim: To encourage children to reach out to others.

Memory Passage: Mark 12:31

Holding Up the Pastor's Hands

Scripture Text: Exodus 17:8-16

   Children can help the pastor.

J=Jesus First
O=Others Second
Y=You Last

 Shop Talk

- ✓ Ask Handy Dan to portray Moses. Go over the Bible story with him, giving him the cues for raising and lowering his hands.
- ✓ Arrange with the pastor's wife (or a family member or someone who knows the pastor well) to come to *kids POWer hour* and answer questions about him. Invite her to stay for the entire session. Borrow one of the pastor's hats for taking the offering. Ask if it is possible for him to come to *kids POWer hour* near the end of the session.
- ✓ Purchase a small gift (such as a corsage) for the interviewee. Choose a child to present it to her. Help the child plan what he or she is going to say. Showing honor by giving is an important lesson which the children need to learn by example.
- ✓ Write review questions from last *kids POWer hour* and this lesson on craft sticks. Place in a jar.
- ✓ The music director should ask the pastor his favorite choruses and be prepared to tape the children singing these songs.
- ✓ Choose a Handy Helper to be the puppeteer during the From Hand to Heart segment. He should plan what he is going to say as a script is not given.
- ✓ Trace around the pastor's right hand and make enough "pastor's hand prints" so each child will have one. Write on each: "I will hold up my pastor's hands by _____."
- ✓ Stretch a line across the front of the room. Make a flashcard of each word of the *POWer line*. With clothespins attach these to the line in jumbled fashion.

Schedule

Date: _____

I. POWer of Worship (25-30 minutes)
  A. Welcome (10 minutes)
    • Getting to Know the Pastor
    • Announcements
  B. Lift Up Holy Hands (3 minutes)
  C. Sing unto the Lord (8 minutes)
    • A Taping Session
  D. Pastor Appreciation (8 minutes)
    • Taped Testimonies
  E. From Our Hands to Yours (3 minutes)
II. POWer of the Word (25-30 minutes)
  A. From Hand to Heart (6 minutes)
    • Puppet Presentation
  B. Worship Chorus (3 minutes)
    • Uplifted Hands
  C. Illustrated Sermon (10 minutes)
    • Holding Up Moses' Hands
  D. Prayer for the Pastor (8 minutes)
  E. Review

On Hand

- ❏ *kids POWer hour* tape
- ❏ tape player
- ❏ *POWer house* papers
- ❏ hand print cutouts
- ❏ clothesline
- ❏ five clothespins
- ❏ flashcards
- ❏ gift for pastor's wife (or interviewee)
- ❏ tacks
- ❏ pastor's hat
- ❏ blank tape
- ❏ craft sticks
- ❏ review notebook
- ❏ joyful gloves and kid's glove
- ❏ puppet
- ❏ Moses' rod and robe
- ❏ a large rock (or small stool covered with brown paper)
- ❏ chalkboard and chalk or dry erase board and markers
- ❏ pencils
- ❏ camera
- ❏ film
- ❏ construction paper cutouts of the pastor's hand
- ❏ small safety pins

> **PLUG-IN:** The earlier children recognize their ability to assist the pastor, the sooner they can benefit the kingdom of God. This lesson takes some coordinating with the pastor and his wife (or a family member), but the results outweigh the inconvenience.

✓ Arrange for a photographer to take a picture of each child with the pastor. If you have a large number of children, take group shots by ages.

POWer of Worship

Welcome (10 minutes)

Handy Dan and his crew welcome the children and help them with the Hands-Full Jars and the attendance chart. Be generous with joyful handshakes.

If one of the pastor's children is in *kids POWer hour*, give him or her the kid's glove to wear.

Work together to unscramble the *POWer line*. **Children can help the pastor.**

Announce that a special guest is coming, the *pastor's wife (or family member)*. Talk briefly about what a good pastor your church has. Tell about a time when he helped your family.

Explain that the *pastor's wife* has agreed to be interviewed in behalf of the pastor. Ask the children what they would like to ask about the pastor. Check for appropriateness and decide which children will ask their questions. These children line up and use the microphone.

Give the *pastor's wife* a standing ovation as she enters. Place her in a special chair in the front of the room for the interview. After the interview have a pre-chosen child present her with a small token of the children's appreciation, such as a corsage.

Lift Up Holy Hands (3 minutes)

In addition to other prayer requests, make a special prayer time for the pastor and his family.

Sing unto the Lord (8 minutes)

Tape the children singing several of the pastor's favorite choruses. An introduction should be recorded first.

This tape was recorded by the *kids POWer hour* choir of the *(church)* on *(date)* in appreciation of their pastor, Brother *(name)*.

Pastor Appreciation (8 minutes)

This portion should also be taped.

Let the children who want to tell about something special the pastor has done for them or why they appreciate him, line up. Limit them to two or three sentences. They should identify themselves and briefly give their testimony. Have a handyman or handmaiden testify first to show the children how. If your group is small and there is time, have a practice taping.

Let the children vote on a child to present the tape to the pastor.

From Our Hands to Yours (3 minutes)

Have the children stand and sing as the pastor's hat is passed for the offering.

POWer of the Word

From Hand to Heart (6 minutes)

Use a puppet to review Mark 12:29-31. The director should stand outside the stage and converse with the puppet. The puppet thinks he knows the memory passage, but he gets terribly confused. Let the children straighten him out.

The children quoting these verses in unison could be added to the tape for the pastor.

Add names to the Recited Memory Passage jar.

Worship Chorus (3 minutes)

Have the children raise their hands over their heads and leave them as long as they can. See how many still have their arms raised after the worship chorus has been sung several times.

ILLUSTRATED SERMON

Holding Up Moses' Hands (10 minutes)

Divide the class into two groups, the Israelites and the Amalekites. Instruct the children that when Moses raises the rod, the Israelites give a shout of victory (not prolonged). When Moses lowers the rod, the Amalekites give a shout of victory. Moses, dressed in a robe and carrying a rod, stands in front of the class beside the teacher. Practice victory shouts a time or two to "adjust volume control."

Show the children where this story is found in their Bibles, Exodus 17. Stress that it really happened.

The Israelites were on their way from Egypt to Canaan when the Amalekites declared war and came out to fight them.

Moses called Joshua, the captain of his army. "Get ready for war," he said. **"Tomorrow I will stand on the top of the hill with the rod of God in my hand so I can watch the battle in the valley."**

The next day Moses took Aaron and Hur with him and went to the top of the hill. Choose "Aaron" and "Hur" to stand beside Moses. **In the valley below the battle raged.**

Moses lifted up his rod. Israelites shout. **Israel drove back the enemy. Then Moses' arm grew tired and he put down the rod.** Amalekites shout. **The Amalekites drove Israel back.**

Moses was worried. He lifted up the rod to God. Israelites shout. **It was strange. Every time he lifted up the rod, the Israelites drove back the enemy. But when his arm grew tired and he let the rod drop, the enemy drove back Israel.** Moses lowers rod and Amalekites shout.

For an hour, two hours, three hours, this happened again and again. Moses raises and lowers the rod a couple of times as the "armies" respond. **Moses was getting awfully tired. But what was he to do? It**

seemed that Israel's winning the battle depended upon Moses keeping the rod up.

Then someone had an idea. It may have been Moses, or Aaron, or Hur. They brought a stone for Moses to sit on. *Boys do so.* Aaron stood on one side of Moses and Hur on the other. They held up Moses' hands until the sun went down. *Israelites shout.*

That day Captain Joshua and his army in the valley won a great victory over the Amalekites because Aaron and Hur held up the hands of the man of God.

Thank your helpers and let them return to their seats.

Who do you think was responsible for Israel's victory? Was it Joshua and the army? Moses? Aaron and Hur? *Let children discuss.* God gave them the victory when everyone worked together.

Holding up someone's hands means "supporting and assisting them." What are some ways children can hold up the pastor's hands or assist him? *Write the children's responses on a board. Answers could include: pray for him, obey him, pick up trash, give him their attention.*

Give each child one of the pastor's hand prints and a pencil. Ask them to make a commitment by choosing one thing from the list and completing the sentence, "I will hold up my pastor's hands by *giving him my attention.*" Handy Helpers and older children should assist the preschoolers. Each child pins the hand print on his lapel.

Children can help the pastor.

Prayer for the Pastor (8 minutes)

If possible, have the pastor come to *kids POWer hour* at this time. As they did with his wife, the children should give him a standing ovation. (Or you may ask permission to take the children into the sanctuary and do this presentation before the adult congregation.)
- Briefly review what you have been studying.
- The elected child presents the tape to the pastor.
- If there is time, let each child verbalize his commitment to support the pastor by stating what he has written on the pastor's hand print. It will help the child keep this commitment if he makes it to the pastor in person.
- Choose two boys to stand beside the pastor and hold up his hands as the children gather around and pray for him.

Review

Let the children take turns drawing a review question from the jar containing the craft sticks. The child drawing the question asks it to the class. He then chooses another child to come forward and draw a question. Have the Hands-Full Jar drawings, including the one for the grand prize.

As the children leave, take each one's picture with the pastor. Have these developed in duplicate, one for the pastor and one for the child.

Give each child a *POWer house* paper as he leaves.

Have you ordered the next *kids POWer hour* manual and tape? If not, order it this week from—
Pentecostal Publishing House
8855 Dunn Road
Hazelwood, MO 63042
Phone 314-837-7300

Unit Three
Character Development

Unit Aim: To help children develop godly qualities in their lives.

Memory Passage: Psalm 134

Lift Up Holy Hands

Prayer Requests

Children love prayer request cards. Make a supply. As the children enter, let them write their requests.

Dan the Handy Man accepts written prayer requests and places them in his toolbox to read during prayer time.

Or a life-sized drawing of Dan could be placed near the door. As the children enter, they write their requests on prayer request cards and affix them to the standup figure. These requests are read during prayer time.

PERMISSION TO COPY

Stand Up for Jesus

Guess Who I Am?

Screen off an area so a mystery testifer can sit behind a screen. A white sheet across a corner with a spotlight behind it will do. The testifier sits behind the sheet and in front of the light so their silhouette shines on the sheet. Lights in the room can be dimmed during the testimony to add mystique.

Put a microphone behind the screen so that everyone can hear the testimony. After the testimony, whoever thinks they can identify the "mystery testifier" must re-state the testimony!

Suggestions are given with each hour's material for how to effectively use this time. Special guests are usually brought in to testify. In a couple of *POWer hours* the children are the "mystery testifiers."

Set a serious "mood" by reminding the children that they must be quiet in order to hear. As soon as the testifier is identified, he or she steps from behind the screen.

Praise the Lord after the testimony!

In three *POWer hours* a costumed Bible character hides behind the screen and gives his testimony to introduce the Illustrated Sermon. The kids will love seeing a costumed Bible character step from behind the screen!

If a screened-off area is not feasible, the "mystery testifier" could testify from a side room using a microphone.

J = Jesus First
O = Others Second
Y = You Last

Unit Three
Character Development

Unit Aim: To help children develop godly qualities in their lives.

Memory Passage: Psalm 134

In God's Hands

Scripture Text: Daniel 3

Stand firm for right.

Schedule

Date: _____

I. POWer of Worship (25-30 minutes)
  A. Welcome (10 minutes)
   • Hands-Full Jars
   • Welcome
   • Hold Tight Demonstration
  B. Lift Up Holy Hands (3 minutes)
   • Prayer Commitments
  C. From Our Hands to Yours (4 minutes)
  D. Sing unto the Lord (5 minutes)
  E. Stand Up for Jesus (5 minutes)
   • Mystery Testifier
II. POWer of the Word (25-30 minutes)
  A. From Hand to Heart (7 minutes)
   • Rewriting the King's English
  B. Worship Chorus (2 minutes)
  C. Illustrated Sermon (15 minutes)
   • The Three Hebrew Children
  D. Invitation and Prayer (5-? minutes)
  E. Review
   • Bible Baseball

Shop Talk

✓ Go over the schedule and this check list with Handy Dan and the crew. Delegate. Delegate. Delegate. Choose one handyman to be the villain. He wears a black cape and half-mask.
✓ Cue the sound effects tape and coordinate it with the sound man.
✓ Make two large stop signs, lettered, "No!" and attach to broomsticks.
✓ Use a paper punch to make a supply of "confetti." Place in a bucket.
✓ For each child make a "No!" stop sign using the pattern on page 65. Glue to craft sticks and place one sign under each chair. Have faith. Make more than you think you will need.
✓ If you have decided to use a life-sized drawing of Handy Dan for prayer requests, construct it and position it in the room.
✓ If an overhead projector is available, make a transparency of the songs, "Stand Right Up for Jesus" and "Behold, Bless Ye the Lord.." Set up the projector so valuable time is not wasted during the session.
✓ Get the "mystery testifier" screen (or room) and microphone ready. Place costume for Nebuchadnezzar behind the screen. Choose an older boy who enjoys laughter to be the king. Give him a copy of his testimony and run though it with him behind the screen to get the correct placement for the light.
✓ Make a crown for King Nebuchadnezzar and use scarves or strips of cloth for turbans for Shadrach, Meshach, Abednego, and the two builder/guards. Add name tags for extra learning.
✓ Copy the POWer house papers.

- ✓ Check the Hands-Full jars. Is there an ample supply of treats, cutout hand prints, and Zip-lok bags?
- ✓ Write the phrases of Psalm 134 on yellow posterboard and the paraphrase version on blue posterboard, as directed under From Hand to Heart.
- ✓ Enlarge and construct the image, using the art on page 125. Disassemble so the students can build it later.
- ✓ Call three or four children who have special testimonies, such as, healing or receiving the Holy Ghost, to be mystery testifiers. Help them word what they are going to say.
- ✓ Add questions to your review notebook.
- ✓ "Pray" your lesson. God will help you know what He wants you to accomplish.

POWer of Worship

On Hand

- ❏ *kids POWer hour* tape
- ❏ tape player
- ❏ *POWer house* papers
- ❏ review notebook
- ❏ black cape and half-mask
- ❏ bucket of confetti
- ❏ paper punch
- ❏ hands-full jars
- ❏ prayer request cards
- ❏ joyful gloves and kid's glove
- ❏ two broomsticks
- ❏ overhead projector
- ❏ transparency of songs, "Stand Right Up for Jesus" and "Behold, Bless Ye the Lord"
- ❏ spotlight
- ❏ screen for Mystery Testifier
- ❏ yellow, red, and blue posterboard
- ❏ craft sticks
- ❏ glue, preferably hot glue
- ❏ crown
- ❏ five scarves or strips of cloth
- ❏ king's robe
- ❏ name tags for head pieces
- ❏ cutout hand prints
- ❏ Zip-loc bags
- ❏ Plasti-Tak

Welcome (10 minutes)

As the children enter, Handy Dan and the Handy Helpers welcome them with joyful handshakes. The crew helps with the Hands-Full Jar activity and the prayer request cards.

Choose two children to help with the "Hold Tight!" Truth Conductor and brief them beforehand. One will be asked to hold a stop sign and the other will be asked to help the one holding the sign. The one holding the sign is to shun any help, saying, "I can hold it myself. I don't need any help." When the villain tries to take the sign, he should let him do so after a brief struggle.

Welcome guests, acknowledge birthdays, and make announcements.

Handy Dan gives the following "Hold Tight!" Truth Conductor.

Aim: We can only hold tight to the right and overcome negative peer pressure by letting God strengthen us. We must accept His help.

Call four children to participate, including the two prechosen ones. Give the two large "No" signs to two of the children, one who has been briefed and one who has not.

Instruct the audience to get the "no" signs from underneath their seats. Tell them to yell "No!" and wave their signs when they think the time is right.

The villain, carrying a bucket of confetti, swoops into the room with his cape flowing. He laughs menacingly! (The children do not know what is in the bucket.) He behaves in a threatening way with it throughout the demonstration.

Ask the other two children to help those with signs hold them. (The children who have been briefed beforehand work together.) Instruct the helpers to wrap their hands around the hands of the ones who are holding the signs, plant their feet, and hold the sign firmly.

The child who was instructed to shun help should start pushing away his helper's hand. He should complain that he can do it without any help.

Turn attention to this child and explain that "danger is lurking around" and he would do well to accept help. Warn him that he is going to have to hold the "No" sign to keep the villain away.

Even as the villain comes closer and closer, laughing hideously, the student refuses help.

The villain swoops down on the child and helper who are strengthening one another. As he threatens to throw the "contents" of his bucket on these children, the students brace their feet and hold on tightly. The audience should be screaming, "No!" and waving their signs.

> **PLUG-IN**: If the congregation yells, "No," to the point it is keeping them from hearing, quiet them. "You're doing a great job yelling 'no,' but wait a minute. I have something important to say to this kid (the one who is refusing help) and I want you to hear what I tell him."

The villain starts to slouch away when he notices the child refusing help. He grins and heads toward him. The child tries to hold the sign, but the villain takes it.

Then the villain laughs and lets this child have it with the confetti!

Let the congregation's reaction die down by itself. If it takes too long, give the crowd control clap. Ask them to put their signs back under their chairs. Save the large signs for later. The helpers can return to their seats.

Satan throws his trash on anyone not strong enough to tell him, "No!" When he comes around and tries to get you to sin, you will not have a sign that says, "No!" But you can use your voice. Or you can just say it in your mind. Even if you have the help of your friends, you are not strong enough to send Satan on his way. You need the help of Someone who is stronger than the enemy. The hand of God is invisible, but His hand is real and strong. Let Him strengthen you so you can say, "No! I will stand firm for right!"

What are you going to say to Satan and sin?

Whose help do we need to strengthen us?

Have the children repeat the *POWer line* several times, increasing volume each time. **Stand firm for right.**

Lift Up Holy Hands (3 minutes)

Handy Dan reads the prayer request cards to the children. As each is read, he asks for a volunteer to come forward and stand in for the one being prayed for. Ask the volunteers to commit to pray for their request each day the coming week. Allow them to keep the prayer request card as a reminder of their commitment.

Lead the children in congregational prayer. Close by asking them to "lift up holy hands" in praise to God who always hears us.

From Our Hands to Yours (4 minutes)

Update the children on the offering project. Let them march and sing as they give.

Count the offering in front of the children and chart it on the graph. Thank them for giving and ask if they have ideas on how they can give more next *kids POWer hour*.

Sing unto the Lord (5 minutes)

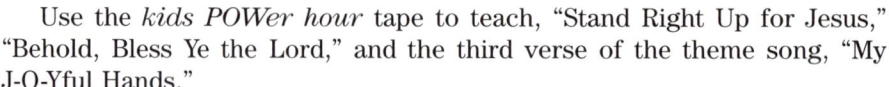

Use the *kids POWer hour* tape to teach, "Stand Right Up for Jesus," "Behold, Bless Ye the Lord," and the third verse of the theme song, "My J-O-Yful Hands."

Allow time for a Dynamo special or two.

Stand Up for Jesus (5 minutes)

Have the three or four prechosen children go behind the screen and stand behind the spotlight. The other children will know who is behind the screen, but they will not know in what order they are going to testify.

The first child picked to testify moves between the spotlight and the screen. After he testifies, the children identify him, and a volunteer restates the testimony. Continue until all mystery testifiers have testified.

Ask the children to give a round of applause to the Lord Jesus as the testifiers return to their seats.

POWer of the Word

From Hand to Heart (7 minutes)

Write these phrases on yellow posterboard flashcards. Write the reference letter faintly so only you can see it.

(a) "Behold,
(b) bless ye the Lord,
(c) all ye servants of the Lord, which by night stand in the house of the Lord.
(d) Lift up your hands in the sanctuary, and bless the Lord. The Lord that made heaven and earth
(e) bless thee
(f) out of Zion."

Write these phrases on blue posterboard. Write the reference letter on the back.

(a) Look here and see!
(b) You kneel down and love and honor God by praising the Lord,
(c) all you worshipers of the Lord which by night stand in the house of the Lord.
(d) Lift up your hands in the church and kneel down and love and honor God by praising the Lord—the Lord that made heaven and earth.
(e) You kneel down and love and honor God by praising the Lord
(f) out of God's special place.

Mix up the blue flashcards. Phrase by phrase help the children get understanding. Lead them in deciding which modern English phrases (blue) could be substituted for the *King James* version (yellow).

> "Behold, bless ye the Lord, all ye servants of the Lord, which by night stand in the house of the Lord. Lift up your hands in the sanctuary, and bless the Lord. The Lord that made heaven and earth bless thee out of Zion."

becomes

> "Look here and see! You kneel down and love and honor God by praising the Lord, all you worshipers of the Lord, which by night stand in the house of the Lord. Lift up your hands in the church, and kneel down and love and honor God by praising the Lord—the Lord that made heaven and earth. You kneel down and love and honor God by praising the Lord out of God's special place."

Work on memorizing the *King James* version.
Not only is the house of the Lord a special place, our hearts are God's special place. We worship God out of our hearts.

Worship Chorus (2 minutes)

As the children sing a worship chorus, the one who is playing the role of King Nebuchadnezzar slips behind the screen and puts on his robe and crown.

If a child does not understand Scriptures that are memorized, he cannot apply them to his life. Let's make sure that the children have understanding with knowledge.

ILLUSTRATED SERMON

The Three Hebrew Children (15 minutes)

> **PLUG-IN** If the children are given an opportunity to sneak a look at the visuals or even play with them, you will lose them during the sermon. You might lose your visuals, too.

The Bible story is introduced by King Nebuchadnezzar giving his testimony. He takes his place between the spotlight and the screen. Children see his shadow.

I was a very powerful king. Flexes muscles.

My army took many prisoners of war, including Daniel and the three Hebrew children.

I was egotist supreme. Taps head. **What's an egotist supreme? Well, it's someone who thinks he's "it"—he's the smartest, the strongest, the best everything. That was me.**

I wanted to be the center of attention all the time. Stands up straight and struts back and forth.

Points up. **Then one day I learned that there is a God in heaven who is the King of all kings—a God who has all power—a God who wants our attention and worship. He sure got my attention when He delivered the three Hebrew children right out of my hand.** Holds out empty hand.

Does anyone know my name? It's a long, hard, strange name.

Turn off the spotlight and let the children guess. If they do not know his name, tell them and have them repeat it after you several times.

Hold an open Bible as you teach. Props needed are the body parts of the image, Plasti-Tak, and a wall or bulletin board on which to build. Choose children to act out the parts. No speaking is necessary, just actions. Help them as you tell the story. Each player should have a headpiece with a name tag. Sound effects of the musical instruments mentioned in Daniel 3 are on the *kids POWer hour* tape.

Show the children how to find Daniel 3. **This is an exciting, true story. If there had been a newspaper back thousands of years ago in Babylon, I'm sure the king would have had this story published in it. Let's ask him. Now what was his name?** Children respond.

Nebuchadnezzar? That's it. Let's call him out here to help tell his story. Children call for him to come from behind the screen. He stands beside you. Each time he is asked a question help him nod his head. The children will enjoy seeing him moved like a marionette.

Is it true that you would have had this story published in the newspaper, King Nebuchadnezzar? Nod his head "yes."

King . . . Oh, what's his name? Children respond. **That's right. King Nebuchadnezzar built a huge idol and set it up in the plain of Dura in Babylon. Is that true, King?** Nod his head "yes." **Nebuchadnezzar called builders to help him set it up because it was hu-mon-gous, gigantic! You did have help, didn't you, King?** Nod his head again.

We need two idol builders. Choose two children to help stick the image parts on the wall or bulletin board. Put turbans on the builders. Save the image's head until last and put it on the end of an arm. **That looks strange. I did it wrong, didn't I?** Nod king's head wildly. **What's wrong, kids?** As the children respond, move the head to the right position.

Okay, the idol is finished. Stand right here, builders, and guard this image. Position one on each side of the idol.

Did your image look like this, King Nebuchadnezzar? Just whisper the answer in my ear. Bend over so the child appears to whisper in your ear. **He said the real image was much, much taller and made of**

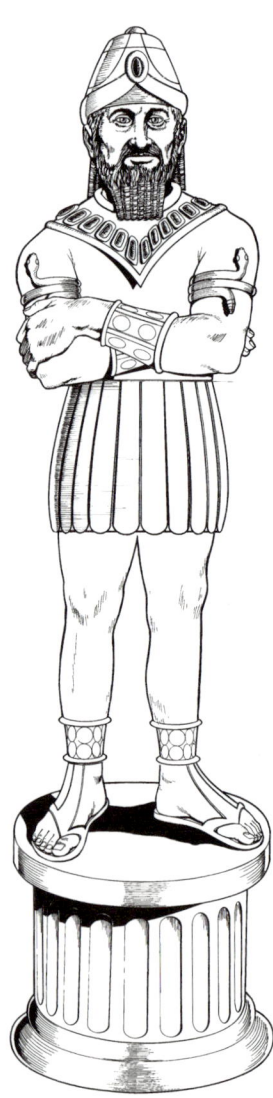

gold! **Tell me in my ear why you built this image, King Nebuchadnezzar.** Bend over and let the child whisper in your ear again.

What do you think he said? Let the children guess. **He built it for the people to worship! There's something not right about that. Why is it wrong to worship idols?** Children respond. **We are to worship only the one true God.**

All the important people in the kingdom were commanded to attend the dedication of the great image. That included three men who had been taken prisoners of war. These guys only worshiped the one true God. Call for three children to be Shadrach, Meshach, and Abednego. Put turbans and name tags on them. Give the two large "No!" signs used during the Truth Conductor to two of the children. The other child stands between them, using his hands to strengthen their grips.

I think I see trouble coming! When were the people to worship the golden image, King Nebuchadnezzar? More whispering. **When the music played?** Nod his head for him. **You mean like this?** Play the *kids POWer hour* sound effects tape. Motion for the "builder/guards" to bow down. The Hebrews stand firm. Stop the tape at the pause. There is a brief lapse before the replay.

These three Hebrew guys said, "No! We will stand firm for right!" They would only worship the one true God. **Did that make you mad, King?** Nod his head violently.

The king threatened to throw them into a fiery furnace if they would not bow down. Even after you threatened to kill them, they refused to bow down, didn't they? Nod his head.

Then Nebuchadnezzar offered them one more chance to change their minds. Okay, we are ready for the music. The music plays. The builder/guards fall down, and the Hebrew three remain standing.

Oh, that made you mad, didn't it? Nod king's head. **So mad that you ordered the furnace heated seven times hotter than it had ever been. Right?** Nod king's head violently. **So you had your strongest guards throw Shadrach, Meshach, and Abednego into the furnace. Did they stand firm for the right, not fearing the heat of the furnace, even though it was seven times hotter than it had ever been?** Nod "yes." **Why?** Let him whisper in your ear. **They would only worship the one true God.**

You know what happened next, kids? Let the children tell you. **That's right. The guards who bound the Hebrews with ropes and threw them into the furnace were killed by the heat.**

When you looked into the fire to see what was happening, King Nebuchadnezzar, what did you see? More whispering.

You saw four men walking in the fire? Four men, unbound, unharmed? God was in the fire with Shadrach, Meshach, and Abednego, and they were not hurt. Their hair was not even singed. Only the ropes which had bound them were burned.

What did this tell you, King Nebuchadnezzar? More whispering. **There is only one God!** More whispering. **And it pays to stand firm for right.** **Everybody shout, "Amen! That's right!"**

Thank your helpers and have them return to their seats. Ask the children to take the "no" signs from under their chairs. Begin labeling the pieces of the idol with things children might worship.

People will try to get you to worship many things—not necessarily an idol like this—but pleasures and possessions. Some might want you to worship drugs by using them. What would you say if someone asked you to use drugs? Encourage the children to wave their signs and shout, "No!"

> **PLUG-IN** Because the three Hebrew children are called "children," we often picture them as kids. Actually they were grown men, descendants of Abraham and therefore called "children."

Some might try to get you to worship rock stars by listening to their music and putting up their posters in your room. What would you say?

Others might want you to smoke, but those who love Jesus say . . . "No! I'll stand firm for right."

Ask the children to help you name more things which might hinder children from worshiping the one true God, such as, sports, movies, alcohol.

Who gave the Hebrew children power to say, "No!" and stand firm for right? Remember the Truth Conductor at the beginning of the hour? We are not strong enough to stand alone for the right, we need God's help.

We will not be thrown into a furnace for standing for right, but our friends can make things "pretty hot" for us when we dare to go against what everyone else is doing.

God protected Shadrach, Meshach, and Abednego from the flames. They were in His hands and that's the safest place in the world. God was in control. We can trust Him to keep us just as He did the Hebrew children.

Ask the children to replace the signs under their chairs and stand quietly.

Invitation and Prayer (5-? minutes)

Musician plays softly.

When we repent of our sins, are baptized in Jesus' name, and receive the Holy Ghost, we have the power of God in us to stand for right.

Invite the children who do not have the Holy Ghost or those who are struggling against peer pressure to come to the front for prayer. Or lead everyone in a prayer similar to this one, having them repeat each phrase after you.

Lord Jesus, please help me to say, "No!" to that villain, Satan, and to the things that would hurt me and separate me from You. Please wrap Your strong hand around mine and lead me the way You want me to go. I trust You to strengthen me while I stand firm for what is right. I am putting my life in Your hands. In Jesus' name. Amen."

Review

Play a simplified game of Bible baseball. To follow all the rules of baseball would be too complicated and time-consuming, so keep it simple.

Set up four chairs around the room for bases. Call the first child to bat. Ask him a question. If he answers correctly, he moves to first base and another child is called to bat. When the second child answers correctly, he moves to first base, the first child moves to second, and so on. If a child cannot answer a question, it is simply an "out." Anytime a child comes "home," he is given a round of applause.

Have the Hands-Full Jar drawing.

Give each child a *POWer house* paper as he leaves. Note that it calls for the children to bring back to the next *POWer hour* a newspaper article about people taking a stand for right. You will need a Special Projects Jar to have a drawing for children who cooperate with this project.

Unit Three
Character Development

Unit Aim: To help children develop godly qualities in their lives.

Memory Passage: Psalm 134

A Sore Thumb

J = Jesus First
O = Others Second
Y = You Last

Scripture Text: I Kings 22:1-37

 Be honest whatever the cost.

Shop Talk

✓ Delegate activities to involve the Handy Helpers and lighten your load.
✓ On a copier that enlarges, make copies of the drawings of the four men in the Bible story (page 75). Color Ahab's crown red and Jehoshaphat's blue.
✓ If an overhead is available, make a transparency of the song, "God Loves Truth."
✓ Add to your notebook a list of true and false statements for voting during the review.
✓ Copy the *POWer house* papers and the puppet script.
✓ Use the pattern on page 127 to make blue construction paper thumb-sized crowns for the thumbs of one-fourth of the children and red crowns for another fourth. The crown should slide down to encircle the base of the thumb. Purchase red adhesive dots for another fourth of the children. The final fourth will be given band-aids. When the children ask, "What's this for?", answer, "Wait and see." Band-aids will be given to every child at the end of the Illustrated Sermon.
✓ Attach the puppet script inside the stage for a guide for puppeteers. Attach a sign, "DO NOT EAT until after supper! Love, Mom" to a cookie jar containing one cookie. Place broken crayons in a large container. (You will find these in the preschool class. Surprise them by trading new crayons for the old.) Use the *kids POWer hour* tape and have a practice session.
✓ Make a special projects Hands-Full Jar for those who return articles showing someone taking a stand for right as suggested in the last *POWer house* paper.
✓ Has someone in your church taken a stand for right against popular opinion—perhaps at school, work, or in the commu-

Schedule
Date: _____

I. POWer of Worship (25-30 minutes)
  A. Welcome (10 minutes)
    • Hands-Full Jar
    • Puppet Skit
    • Announcements
  B. Sing unto the Lord (6 minutes)
  C. Lift Up Holy Hands (4 minutes)
  D. A Lesson from the Toolbox (3 minutes)
    • Magnetic Truth Conductor
  E. Stand Up for Jesus (4 minutes)
    • Mystery Testifier

II. POWer of the Word (25-30 minutes)
  A. From Hand to Heart (8 minutes)
    • Puzzle Teams
  B. Worship Chorus (2 minutes)
  C. Illustrated Sermon (10 minutes)
    • Micaiah and the False Prophets
  D. Invitation and Prayer (5-? minutes)
  E. Review
    • Thumbs Up, Thumbs Down

On Hand

- ❏ *kids POWer hour* tape
- ❏ tape player
- ❏ *POWer house* papers
- ❏ Hands-Full Jars, cutout hand prints, Zip-loc™ bags
- ❏ joyful gloves and kid's glove
- ❏ thumb splint and tape
- ❏ screen and spotlight
- ❏ review notebook
- ❏ prayer request cards
- ❏ overhead projector and transparencies of songs, optional
- ❏ red sticker dots (the kind used to color code files)
- ❏ red and blue construction paper thumb-sized crowns
- ❏ band-aids
- ❏ two puppets
- ❏ copy of puppet script
- ❏ cookie jar and one cookie
- ❏ large container of broken crayons
- ❏ magnet
- ❏ miscellaneous metal objects
- ❏ miscellaneous plastic, wood, paper items
- ❏ colored posterboard
- ❏ rubber cement
- ❏ damp cloth
- ❏ small prizes
- ❏ robe and crown
- ❏ trash cans

nity? Ask this person to be your "mystery testifer," and tell about their experience. They should be in place behind the screen before the children arrive.

✓ Choose an older boy or handyman to give Ahab's mystery testimony.

✓ For each team of two to eight (depending upon the size of your group), make a memory passage puzzle. Write Psalm 134 on colored posterboard (a different color for each team). Cut into a puzzle with each piece containing one word or phrase. Each puzzle should have the same number of pieces.

✓ Copy the prize stamp art from page 74 to make stickers to give the winners of the memory passage game. Coat the back with rubber cement and let dry. Cut out. To apply as a sticker, moisten the back with a damp cloth.

POWer of Worship

Welcome (10 minutes)

Handy Dan has a splint on the thumb of his dominant hand. He "pretends" to have hit it with a hammer. As he welcomes the children and gives his Lesson from the Toolbox, he should make a big issue out of having a "sore thumb."

The Handy Helpers welcome the children with joyful handshakes, and help with the Hands-Full Jar activity and prayer request cards. The children who bring an article showing someone taking a stand for right put their name on a hand print and place it in the special projects jar for an extra drawing at the end of the session. If only one child remembered, let him wear the kid's glove.

As Handy Dan visits with the children, he watches for things to fix (feelings, smilers, etc.) and passes out "prescriptions" (Scripture references) from his Bible.

Place blue and red crowns, red adhesive dots, and band-aids on a table. As the children enter, the first child is given a blue crown, the second a red, the third a red dot, and the fourth a band-aid; repeat. This is a simple way to divide into fourths.

Start with a surprise—a puppet skit.

Fibs are Lies

Cookie jar with the sign and without the lid sits on the edge of the puppet stage. One puppeteer is needed to handle the props.

ENTER BOY, looks at cookie jar.

BOY: Reads. **"Do not eat until after supper. Love, Mom."** Peeks into the jar. **Yummm, that cookie looks so good—smells good, too.** He looks around. **No one is watching. No one will ever know.** Sneaks a cookie and gobbles it up noisily.

EXIT BOY. After a short pause, ENTER BOY, carrying a large container of broken crayons. Fumbles through them frantically.

ENTER GIRL.

GIRL: **What are you doing? You look like you need help.**

BOY: Continues to dig without looking up. **I do. Will you help me? I need a certain crayon out of this box.**

GIRL: Helps dig. Easily picks out a crayon—any color but white. **Here. Here's a crayon.** Whispers aside to audience. **I don't know what was so hard about that. He's got a whole box of crayons!**

BOY: Continues to dig. **Thanks, that's a nice color, but it won't work. I need a white crayon and I need it in a hurry.**

Puppets throw crayons into the air as they hurriedly hunt through the container.

GIRL: **What are you in such a hurry to color?**

BOY: **A fib I'm getting ready to tell Mom.**

GIRL:	What? You don't need a white crayon. You can't color fibs.	BOY:	Interrupts. **Oh, now I remember.** Joins Girl singing. "Fibs are lies, and lies are lies; No difference in between."
BOY:	Yes, I can. Haven't you ever heard of "little white fibs"? I ate a cookie and Mom's going to ask about it because it was the last cookie in the jar. I'm going to tell her that I don't know who ate it. It's not a lie, just a little white fib.		Stops singing abruptly. **But what should I tell Mom? Just one itty, bitty fib—I mean, lie—and I won't get in trouble.**
GIRL:	Whoa! Hold on there! Don't you remember what we learned at *kids POWer hour?* Did you forget?	GIRL:	Sighs heavily. **You'd better tell the truth because God loves the truth and He hates a lie!** Remember our *POWer line* for today is "Be honest whatever the cost."
BOY:	Stops digging through crayons and scratches head. **I guess I did. Remind me.** Hold up hand. **Wait. On second thought, maybe I don't want you to remind me.**	BOY:	**You're right. I'm sorry I even thought about telling a lie.**
GIRL:	We learned that there are no little bitty, white fibs. **Fibs are lies, and lies are lies.** Sings to the tune, "Mares Eat Oats." "Fibs are lies, and lies are lies; No difference in between."	BOTH:	Sing. "Fibs are lies, and lies are lies; No difference in between. Good kids tell all lies, 'Good-bye,' And so should I."
			EXIT PUPPETS. PERMISSION TO COPY SCRIPT

Have the children repeat after you the *POWer line*: **Be honest whatever the cost.**

Welcome guests, make announcements, and acknowledge birthdays.

Sing unto the Lord (6 minutes)

Teach the children the new song, "God Loves the Truth." If you know the song "The Hebrew Boys" from The Winner's Series *kids POWer hour* tape, this would be a good time to review it. To save time, take up the offering during the praise choruses. Have a Handy Helper count and record it.

For the Dynamo Special choose two or three children to be the "Praise Singers," and let them lead the singing. Use shy children who are reluctant to sing solos. This is a good confidence builder.

Lift Up Holy Hands (4 minutes)

Ask how many children remembered their commitment from last *kids POWer hour*. Does anyone have a "praise report" to give for answered prayer?

Handy Dan reads the prayer requests from his toolbox and leads the children in prayer. If there is time, pray for each request individually.

A Lesson from the Toolbox (3 minutes)

Handy Dan gives this Truth Conductor, making a big issue out of how awkward it is to have "a sore thumb."

Scatter miscellaneous metal, plastic, paper, and wooden items on a table. Show the children a magnet and discuss how it attracts only items containing metal.

Just as a magnet draws objects containing metal, God draws those who have a love for the truth to Himself. Read, or have an older child read, Proverbs 12:22.

God hates lying. It is repulsive to Him, but He delights in the truth and those who tell the truth.

Read, or have a child read, I Thessalonians 4:16-17. **At the Rapture, Jesus will draw those who love and obey the truth up to meet Him in the air. Those who do not love and obey the truth will be left behind.**

> To involve the children, write Scripture references on index cards. Give to older children who enjoy reading aloud. Ask them to find the verse and be prepared to read it.

The Holy Ghost, which is the Spirit of Truth, will draw us up to meet the Lord in the air. If you want to be caught up in the Rapture, you must have the Holy Ghost. Read Romans 8:11.

Stand Up for Jesus (4 minutes)

Turn the spotlight on the "Mystery Testifier." After he has given his testimony and been identified, allow the children who brought articles of people standing up for right to briefly share their findings.

POWer of the Word

From Hand to Heart (8 minutes)

Ask the children to open their Bibles to the middle. They should be in or near the Book of Psalms. Find and read together Psalm 134. Repeat, if needed, to acquaint children with the passage.

Divide into teams of two to eight—one team per puzzle. Assign each team a color. Designate preschoolers and the remaining children as cheerleaders for specific teams and include them in the prizes, should their team win.

At one end of the room, place all the puzzle pieces in a big pile. Designate a place for each team to construct their puzzle (could be on a table or wall).

Teams line up. At the "go" signal, the first player on each team runs to the pile of puzzle pieces and finds the piece of his team's color with the first word or phrase of the memory passage on it. He places it in his designated construction spot and tags the next person on his team. The second player puts the second piece in place, etc. All the while, the team members cheer and root for their team. If a player thinks that someone before him has made a mistake, he can correct it.

Award prize stamps to the first and second place teams. Be sure the children understand that these will be traded for their prize at the end of *kids POWer hour*.

Worship Chorus (2 minutes)

As the children sing a worship chorus to prepare their hearts for the Word of the Lord, the one chosen to give Ahab's testimony steps behind the screen and puts on a robe and crown.

ILLUSTRATED SERMON

Micaiah and the False Prophets (10 minutes)

"King Ahab" moves in front of the spotlight behind the screen to give his testimony. He stands sideways with his profile spotlighted.

I was one of the most wicked kings ever to rule in Israel, but I was not as wicked as my wife. My, she was a terror! Trembles and shakes. **She worshiped Baal and threatened to kill the prophet Elijah**

Hooray!
You're a
FIRST PLACE WINNER

Trade this stamp for a prize as you leave *kids POWer hour*.

Yeah!
SECOND PLACE

Trade this stamp for a prize as you leave *kids POWer hour*.

Prize stamps/stickers are traded for prizes as the children leave. They serve three purposes: (1) the child gets an immediate reward for being a winner, (2) they will not eat or play with their prize during *kids POWer hour*, and (3) others will not be distracted.

because he served the one true God. She is best known for painting her face. Makes motions as if painting his face.

Once I got mad and pouted like a three-year-old because my neighbor would not sell me his garden. Pushes out lips and sticks out tongue. My cunning little wife got it for me when she had the man killed.

I was killed in battle by an unknown soldier who shot an arrow into the air. Makes motion of arrow flying through the air and piercing his heart.

My name starts with the first letter of the alphabet and ends with the second. It rhymes with "gab."

Turn off the spotlight. Can anyone identify the mystery testifier? If not, give them another chance after the Illustrated Sermon.

We are going to learn about some rich and famous people. Turn in your Bible to I Kings 22. Show the children how to find it. Older children should help the younger. Guess how two of the men in today's story became rich and famous. I'll give you a clue. What is the name of the book of the Bible where we find the story? Help the children connect that the men were kings.

Call for two children to hold the drawings of Ahab and Jehoshaphat. Identify the kings and have the children repeat their names a few times. Instruct the children with red crowns on their thumbs that they are to wave their thumbs each time they hear the name "Ahab," and the child holding the drawing of Ahab is to raise it as high as he can. The ones with the blue crowns and the child holding the picture of Jehoshaphat do the same when they hear his name. Practice by saying these names a couple of times. The action names are in italics in the lesson text.

Jehoshaphat and *Ahab* were kings. *Ahab* was king of Israel. What was his wife's name? Jezebel. Did you ever hear about the time when *Ahab* and Jezebel's four hundred and fifty prophets of Baal built an altar and had a contest with the God of Elijah on Mount Carmel? The prophets of Baal prayed and cried and cut themselves trying to get Baal's attention, but nothing happened. Do you know why? Let the children respond.

When Elijah, the prophet of the true God, prayed, God sent down fire and consumed the altar and the sacrifice. The false prophets of *Ahab* were killed, but there were four hundred more prophets which were not killed. *Ahab* was an extremely wicked king who did not love or honor the true God. What was this wicked king's name?

Jehoshaphat was king of Judah and *Ahab*'s neighbor. What was the name of the king of Judah?

Jehoshaphat loved and served the one true God. He did many good things, but he made one bad mistake. *Jehoshaphat* decided to go along with a plan of King *Ahab*. Why do you think it was not a good idea for a king who loved God to go along with a king who did not love God? Let the children discuss.

Jehoshaphat should not have made an alliance (or an agreement) with *Ahab*, but he did. Here's how it happened.

One day *Jehoshaphat* went to visit *Ahab*. *Ahab* was mad at the king of Syria. He said to *Jehoshaphat*, "Will you go with me to fight and take back the city of Ramoth-gilead?"

That's when *Jehoshaphat* should have said, "No way." Instead he said, "I am with you and my soldiers are your soldiers. My horses are your horses." Huh-oh! Trouble coming!

Ahab grinned. He may have even laughed!

Then *Jehoshaphat* remembered something. "First we need to ask the Lord."

That wiped the grin off *Ahab*'s face. He knew that the true prophets of God, like Elijah, heard from God and spoke only what

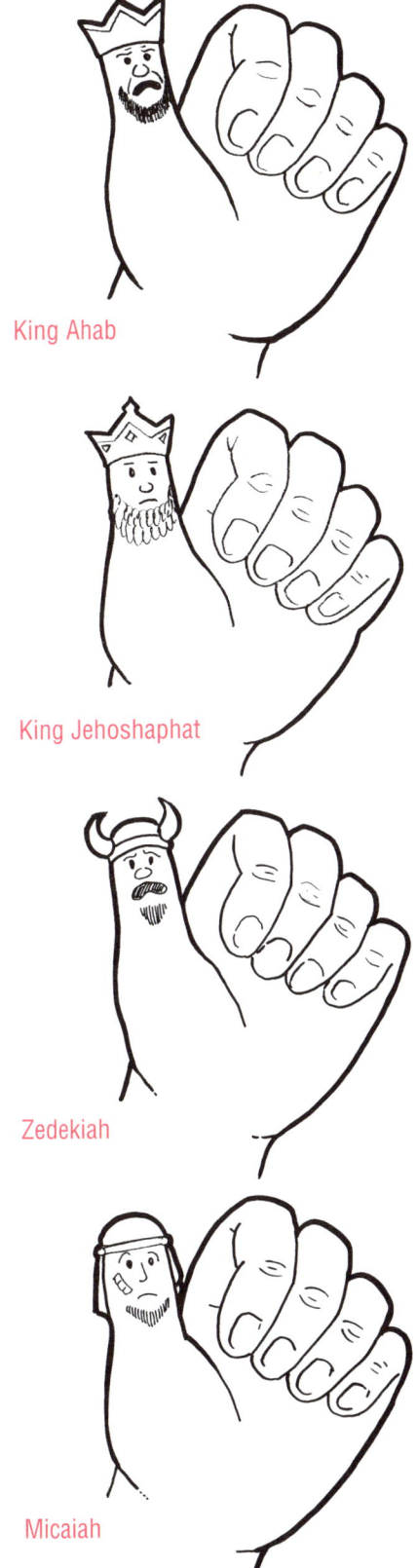

King Ahab

King Jehoshaphat

Zedekiah

Micaiah

God told them. What a true prophet said always came to pass. *Ahab* did not like the true prophets because they would not say what he wanted them to. They said what God told them to, whether the king liked it or not.

So *Ahab* called for his false prophets, some four hundred of them.

One of the false prophets was Zedekiah. Call for another child to hold up the drawing of Zedekiah. Instruct the children with red dots on their thumbs, as well as the one with the picture, to hold them up when you say, "Zedekiah." **Let's practice. What was the false prophet's name?** *Zedekiah.* **Great!**

What does "false" mean? Children respond. **False is something that is not true; it is a lie. False prophets were lying prophets.** *Zedekiah* **was a lying prophet.**

Ahab asked his false prophets, "Shall I go to war against Ramoth-gilead or not?" All the lying prophets screamed, "Go, for the Lord will give the city to you." *Zedekiah* went to great lengths to illustrate his lie. He made iron horns and told the kings, "This is what the Lord says: 'With these horns you will gore the people of Ramoth-gilead until they are destroyed.'"

Jehoshaphat felt very, very uncomfortable. Something was not quite right. He must have felt like your mother does when your brother or sister tells her a lie. Of course, you do not lie, do you? Oops, watch it. Don't tell another one.

Was *Zedekiah* **telling the truth?** Children respond. **How do you know?** Because he was a lying prophet and not interested in the truth.

King *Jehoshaphat* was uneasy! He asked, "Is there not a prophet of the Lord that we could ask?" He knew these four hundred men were not God's prophets.

Reluctantly, King *Ahab* said, "Well, we could call Micaiah, but I hate him. He never prophesies anything good about me."

Jehoshaphat rebuked him and said, "You should not say that you hate *Micaiah*. Bring him here."

Call for another child to hold up the drawing of Micaiah and have the children with the band-aids on their thumbs identify with the drawing in the same way the others have been doing. Test their understanding by saying, "Micaiah," a couple of times while they hold up the drawing and their thumbs.

A messenger went to bring *Micaiah* to *Ahab* and *Jehoshaphat*. The lying prophet *Zedekiah* stayed around to see what would happen.

Micaiah was a true prophet. He never lied, no matter what the consequences. The messenger warned *Micaiah* that if he wanted to stay out of trouble, he would have to lie. He told him that all the other prophets were telling the kings what they wanted to hear—to go to war, and that they would win.

Micaiah replied, "As surely as the Lord lives, I will tell *Ahab* only what the Lord tells me."

Even before *Micaiah*, the true prophet, came face to face with *Zedekiah*, the false prophet, he was pressured to tell a lie. But *Micaiah* did not fail God.

He was determined to "be honest whatever the cost."

Micaiah knew that it was more important to please God than to please two rich and famous kings. *Micaiah* knew that *Ahab* hated him! He knew that he would probably suffer for telling the truth, but *Micaiah* told the truth anyway.

God loves truth. He hates lies. Satan is the father (or inventor) of lies. Anyone who tells lies is obeying Satan and displeasing God.

So *Micaiah* told the truth. "I saw the armies of Israel scattered without a leader." Meaning, they were going to lose the battle. Wow!

It took a lot of courage to tell the kings, "Don't go to war. You're going to lose," after four hundred prophets had said, "Go. You're going to win."

Then *Micaiah* went on to tell the kings that *Zedekiah* and his fellow prophets had a lying spirit.

When *Zedekiah* heard *Micaiah's* message, he almost exploded! He was so angry he slapped *Micaiah* while *Ahab* and *Jehoshaphat* watched.

Ahab ordered, "Put *Micaiah* in prison. Feed him on bread and water until we return from the battle in peace."

Micaiah looked the wicked king in the eye. "If you come home in peace, everyone will know that the Lord hasn't spoken to me."

Micaiah was punished for telling the truth, but he would not change his message because it was true.

Despite what *Micaiah* had warned, *Jehoshaphat* went to war with *Ahab*. What do you think happened? They lost. King *Ahab* put on a disguise so no one would recognize him as the king of Israel, but God knew who he was and where he was. An unknown soldier put an arrow in his bow and shot it. The arrow went straight to the chariot where Ahab sat and struck him. He died. How sad that he would not listen to the truth.

Micaiah was pressured to lie and suffered for the truth, but he pleased God. He was the winner.

Collect the pictures and thank your helpers as they return to their seats.

Hold up the picture of Ahab. Brainstorm to draw from the children reasons they do not want to be like King Ahab. Ask them to remove the red crowns from their thumbs and wad them up. Have the Handy Helpers ready with trash cans to collect them.

Hold up Zedekiah's picture and ask why they would not want to be like him. Have them remove the red dots from their thumbs and throw them away.

Show Jehoshaphat's picture. Discuss why they would not want to be like him, even though he loved God and was a good king most of the time. Have them remove the blue crowns from their thumbs.

Show the drawing of Micaiah. Talk about why it pays to be like him even though he stood out like "a sore thumb." Give each child a band-aid to put on their thumb as a reminder to be like Micaiah who dared to be honest.

At this time Handy Dan should remove the splint from his thumb and tell the children that he is going to be completely honest with them. He explains that he really did not have a sore thumb. He merely wanted the children to realize what it means to be "a sore thumb."

A sore thumb is awkward and "stands out." Often children who tell the truth and do what is right "stand out" and feel "awkward." But we must "be honest whatever the cost."

Invitation and Prayer (5-? minutes)

As the musician plays softly, ask the children to stand.

Hold up your Bible. **The Word of God is the truth. Every word in it is true. It tells us how to be saved. We must repent, be baptized in Jesus' name, and receive the Holy Ghost. Satan lies to people and tells them they can be saved another way. But there is no other way.**

Right now Satan may be whispering lies in your mind. "If you live for Jesus, you'll be a sore thumb. You'll stick out and be different from everybody else." "You don't want to pray today. You can pray later when you're older." Don't listen to his lies.

If the children did not guess Ahab's identity as the mystery testifier, repeat Ahab's testimony now and let them guess again.

Is your next *kids POWer hour* manual in hand? Because this curriculum is undated, you could be using any of the kPh books. Whatever the series, it is time to read the feature pages and decide which activities will work in your situation. Set a date for a staff work night and start announcing it.

Do you feel the Spirit of God pulling you toward Him like a magnet draws metal objects? Today is the day of salvation. The Lord wants to fill you with His Spirit right here, right now. Will you come and pray?

Review

Have "thumbs up, thumbs down" voting. Make a statement and let the children vote as to whether or not it is true. True—thumbs up. False—thumbs down.

Sample statements might be: *Jesus always told the truth. A little white fib is okay now and then. The devil loves the truth.* Make this activity minister to your children by making statements pertinent to situations in their lives.

Have the Hands-Full Jars drawing.

Give each child a *POWer house* paper as he leaves. Let winners trade in their stamp/stickers for prizes.

Faith Tabernacle of La Marque, Texas, under the leadership of Sister Teresa Bohannon, shows what can be done with imagination, initiative, and an overhead projector. The hanging tools are sofa cushions she salvaged from an abandoned couch put out as trash! Be on the lookout for your own great "buys!"

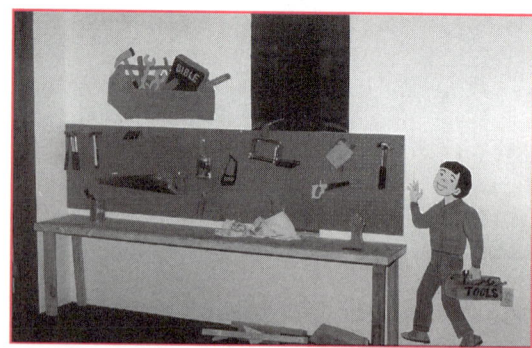
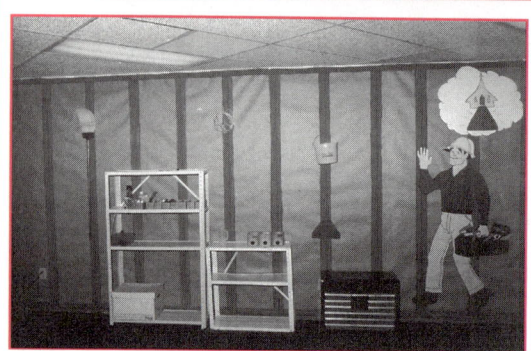

Unit Three
Character Development

Unit Aim: To help children develop godly qualities in their lives.

Memory Passage: Psalm 134

J = Jesus First
O = Others Second
Y = You Last

Idle Hands

Scripture Text: II Kings 7; Ecclesiastes 9:10; Proverbs 18:9

 Do what you can.

 Shop Talk

✓ Check the Hands-Full Jars. Next *kids POWer hour* will be the final grand drawings. Do you have enough prizes?
✓ On posterboard, copy the masks of Slothful, Sluggard, Diligence, and Zeal (pages 80-81), using faint lines which cannot be seen by the children. As you tell the story, color in the lines with markers.
✓ Make four paving blocks by folding newspapers and wrapping them in brown paper bags. On each block write one of the following: repent, be baptized in Jesus' name, receive the Holy Ghost, live a holy life.
✓ Give the sound man the *kids POWer hour* tape and a copy of the Illustrated Sermon. Practice the timing with him.
✓ For each child make a flashcard which reads, "Lazy Hands" on one side and "Working Hands" on the other. Place a sign under each chair.
✓ On scraps of posterboard write the words of the memory passage which are replaced by sound effects on the *kids POWer hour* tape. (See From Hand to Heart.) Make one set for each team. If you have a large group, have two teams. If your group is small, have enough teams of two to four children to involve everyone. (For added interest, add some words which were not omitted from the recording. To be fair make each set identical.)
✓ Make copies of the *POWer house* papers.
✓ Arrange for someone who works with their hands to give the mystery testimony. They could talk about how the Lord led them into their area of work and the satisfaction they get from

Schedule
Date: _____

I. POWer of Worship (25-30 minutes)
  A. Welcome (7 minutes)
    • Hands-Full Jars
    • Mystery Testifier
    • *POWer line* Rebus
  B. Visualized Story (6 minutes)
    • Slothful and Sluggard Meet Diligence and Zeal
  C. Sing unto the Lord (6 minutes)
    • Praise Choruses
    • Memory Specials
  D. Lift Up Holy Hands (4 minutes)
    • Echo Praise Break
    • Prayer Requests
  E. From Our Hands to Yours (4 minutes)
II. POWer of the Word (25-30 minutes)
  A. From Hand to Heart (8 minutes)
    • Missing Words
  B. Worship Chorus (3 minutes)
  C. Illustrated Sermon (10 minutes)
    • Four Lepers of Samaria
  D. Invitation and Prayer (5-? minutes)
  E. Review
    • Pictionary™

On Hand

- ❏ *kids POWer hour* tape
- ❏ tape player
- ❏ *POWer house* papers
- ❏ newspapers
- ❏ brown paper bags
- ❏ set of markers
- ❏ posterboard
- ❏ wheelbarrow or lawn cart
- ❏ dry erase board and markers or chalkboard and chalk
- ❏ mystery testifier screen and light
- ❏ overhead projector, transparency (optional)

Slothful

Sluggard

 PLUG-IN Pretending to "forget" names helps to reinforce them in the children's minds. They will easily catch on that your memory is not that bad and fall right in with your game.

working with their hands. This person needs to be in place behind the screen before the children arrive.

✓ If an overhead is available, make a transparency of the *POWer line* rebus. Otherwise, draw the rebus on a board and cover until time to decode it.

POWer of Worship

Welcome (7 minutes)

Handy Dan and the Handy Helpers greet the children with big smiles and joyful handshakes. They help with the Hands-Full Jars activity and prayer request cards.

Start by singing the theme song, "My J-O-Yful Hands." Welcome guests, acknowledge birthdays, and make announcements.

Let the mystery testifier give his testimony so he can come out from behind the screen.

Place the *POWer line* rebus transparency on an overhead. Or uncover the one on the board. Let the children work together to decode it.

Repeat several times: **Do what you can.**

Slothful and Sluggard Meet Diligence and Zeal
(6 minutes)

Place the building blocks in a wheelbarrow or lawn cart and set to one side of the room. As you tell the story, four children will hold the masks.

Once upon a time long, long ago there were two brothers, Slothful and Sluggard. What were their names?

One brother was Slothful and the other was . . . oh, my! What was his name?

Once upon a time long, long ago there were two brothers. Their names were Sluggard and . . . oh, what was the first one's name?

I've got it—Slothful and Sluggard. They were brothers.

Slothful and Sluggard had two cousins—two brothers named Diligence and Zeal. What were the cousins' names?

Do you want to see what they looked like? Call four children to hold the masks. Wait until you start to describe a character before giving the mask to a child to hold. Darken the lines on each mask as you describe the character so it appears you are drawing it. Start with Slothful.

As you can see, Slothful was not a happy person. He was slow and inactive—that means, he didn't move around much. He didn't even comb his hair this morning—probably because he stayed in bed until noon. Look at his eyes. He did not like to open them. He was afraid he would see something that he should have been doing. Slothful made himself unhappy, but he was too lazy to change his ways.

Sluggard was very much like his brother, Slothful. His hair was a different color, but just as messy! That's because he stayed in bed until after noon. He wasn't a bit happy when he had to get up.

No one could depend on . . .what were their names?

Slothful and Sluggard did not have many friends. If anyone asked them to do something, they would say, "Yes, we will do it for you," but they never got around to doing it. Usually, though, if anyone asked them to do something, they said, "We don't want to. It's too hard. We don't even want to try."

If Slothful and Sluggard wanted anything, they looked for the easiest way to get it, even if it meant being dishonest.

Remember the other two brothers—the cousins? What were their names?

Diligence was a happy camper! He kept busy. He got up early every morning to read his Bible and pray.

Zeal was much like his brother, Diligence. He got up early, too, eager to find out what excitement the day had in store.

Diligence and Zeal were not afraid of hard work. They could be depended upon to keep their word and get the job done. Diligence and Zeal were honest, too.

Diligence

Zeal

Ask the children to get the signs out from under their chairs. Have one child stand and read both sides. Point to one of the brothers and have the children hold up the sign—with the words pointing toward the front—which they think is applicable to him. Instruct them that when you name the brothers, they are to hold up the matching sign. Cues are in italics in the text.

Once upon a time there were two brothers, *Slothful and Sluggard.*

At noon one day the king came to *Slothful and Sluggard* **and asked them to build a road to a far away beautiful city. What do you think the king found** *Slothful and Sluggard* **doing? Right. They were sleeping.** Have the boys holding these signs snore.

The king was not pleased. Tape recording of thunder. **He woke them up.** Tape of king's voice. "Wake up! I have come to ask you to build a road to a far away, beautiful city so many will be able to travel there to live with me. I have supplied the necessary paving stones, but I need your hands to work." Have someone bring the wheelbarrow of paving stones to the front.

Slothful and Sluggard **whined, "We are much too tired to work." And they went back to sleep. The king was greatly displeased.** Tape recording of thunder.

He went down the road to where *Diligence and Zeal* **lived. Do you think he found them sleeping?**

Diligence and Zeal **had already prayed and read their Bibles. They were helping their parents with the chores. The king liked what he saw in these brothers. He made his request to them.** Tape of king's voice. "I have come to ask you to build a road to a far away, beautiful city so many will be able to travel there to live with me. I have supplied the necessary paving stones, but I need your hands to work."

Diligence and Zeal **told the king, "We will . . .** point at the *POWer line* for the children to repeat . . . **do what we can." They began work on the road at once.** Pick up one of the paving stones, pretending it is heavy. **The paving stones were heavy. At times the sharp edges scraped their hands, but** *Diligence and Zeal* **kept working. They did their best to obey the king's orders. They worked with enthusiasm until the job was done. As they placed the last stone in the roadway, the king said . . .** Tape of king's voice, "Well done, Diligence and Zeal. You will live with me forever!"

Slothful and Sluggard **had lost out.** *Diligence and Zeal* **were rewarded.**

Collect masks and thank your helpers. The children should place their flashcards back under their chairs. This story will be brought into the Illustrated Sermon.

Sing unto the Lord (6 minutes)

Let the children request their favorite choruses from this series.

For the Dynamo Special emphasize memory work. Ask for a couple of volunteers to recite special Scripture passages.

Lift Up Holy Hands (4 minutes)

Read together Psalm 47:1: *"O clap your hands, all ye people; shout unto God with the voice of triumph."*

Teach the children to obey this verse. Give the Lord a round of applause. Then have an "echo" praise break. Instruct them to echo each praise phrase as you shout it "with the voice of triumph."

After a time of praise, ask Handy Dan to read the prayer requests and lead the children in congregational prayer.

From Our Hands to Yours (4 minutes)

Ask for a show of "working" hands. **In the last week how many have worked? Tell us what you did.** It may have been making a bed, carrying out the trash, washing dishes. Ask if they know a way they can make some money before the next *kids POWer hour*. Are they willing to give part or all of what they make to the special project? Get from them a commitment to work and give.

Ask the children who have more than one piece of money to share with those around them who do not have anything to give. As a lively march tune plays, let the children march and give.

Count and record the offering so all can see.

POWer of the Word

From Hand to Heart (8 minutes)

Divide the children into teams. Place each team's stack of word cards (made as instructed under **Shop Talk**) on a table in front of them.

Play the *kids POWer hour* tape, pushing the pause button each time a sound effect is heard.

The team members, working quietly so as not to clue the other team in, decide which word was omitted and hold up the appropriate card. As soon as a team holds up the correct word, the tape is started. A scorekeeper is needed.

Behold, bless ye the SOUND EFFECT, *all ye* SOUND EFFECT *of the* LORD, *which by* SOUND EFFECT *stand in the* SOUND EFFECT *of the* LORD.

Lift up your SOUND EFFECT *in the sanctuary, and* SOUND EFFECT *the* LORD.

The LORD *that made* SOUND EFFECT *and earth bless thee out of* SOUND EFFECT.

Worship Chorus (3 minutes)

Lead the children in some worship choruses to prepare their hearts for the Word of the Lord.

The Lepers of Samaria (10 minutes)

Ask questions to review the story of Slothful and Sluggard. Explain that this is "just a story," which has a lesson to teach us. Emphasize that Bible stories are not made up. They are true.

Open your Bibles to II Kings 7. Show the children how to find it. **In this chapter is a story about four men who had to decide whether to be like Slothful and Sluggard or Diligence and Zeal. It was a matter of life or death for them.**

There was a great famine in Samaria. What is a famine? Let children respond.

There was no food because the enemy had surrounded them. They had no way to get food. The people were starving.

One day the prophet Elisha came to the people and said. . . . Play the *kids POWer hour* tape. *"Hear ye the word of the LORD; Thus saith the LORD, To morrow about this time shall a measure of fine flour be sold for a shekel, and two measures of barley for a shekel, in the gate of Samaria."*

What does that mean? Let's listen again. Play the next segment of tape which is a paraphrase of Elisha's words. *"Hear the Word of the LORD! Today you have nothing to eat and you are very, very hungry; but tomorrow there will be so much to eat in Samaria that you will be able to buy flour to make bread and grain to eat for just a little money."* Sound of people laughing.

Though the people were hungry, they laughed because they did not believe there would be lots of food the next day. All they believed was what they saw—zero food to eat. They had no faith in God or the man of God, Elisha.

One man was like Slothful and Sluggard. He was an important man in the king's government. He said to Elisha. . . . Play tape. *"Even if God made windows in heaven, there would not be that much food poured out by tomorrow."*

Elisha was angered by the man's lack of faith. He told him. . . . Play tape. *"You will see the food tomorrow, but you will not eat any of it."*

In Samaria were four other men—men who had crippled hands. It was difficult for these men to work because they had leprosy. They were not even allowed inside the city. As they sat outside the gate, they decided they could sit there and starve or they could do something. What they decided to do was go to the enemy's camp where they knew there was food and beg for mercy. Here's what they said. Play tape. *"Why sit we here until we die? If we say, We will enter into the city, then the famine is in the city, and we shall die there: and if we sit still here, we die also. Now therefore come, and let us fall unto the host of the Syrians: if they save us alive, we shall live; and if they kill us, we shall but die."*

These men were like Diligence and Zeal. They decided to do what they could.

As the sun went down, they got up and started to the enemy's camp to find food. While they were walking toward the camp, God amplified the sound of their footsteps. The enemy thought they heard a mighty army approaching. It sounded something like this. Play tape of approaching army.

God worked a miracle on the enemy's ears. The enemy jumped up and ran from camp as fast as they could. Guess what they left when they ran? Everything! They left their tents, their horses, their donkeys, their silver and gold, their clothes, and most important of all, their food!

Pray your Illustrated Sermon. As you commune with God about the content, He will help you relax, get the delivery in your mind, and be sensitive to the needs of the children.

When the lepers came to the camp, their eyes got bigger and bigger as they went from tent to tent. They ate and drank until they were stuffed. They carried out silver and gold and clothes and hid it. They carried out more silver and gold and clothes and hid it.

Then they remembered their family and friends. One said. . . . Play tape. *"We do not well: this day is a day of good tidings, and we hold our peace: if we tarry till the morning light, some mischief will come upon us: now therefore come, that we may go and tell the king's household."*

The four crippled men did what they could. They returned to the city and told everyone the good news. The next day the people traveled the road to the enemy's camp. Just as Elisha had spoken, there was lots and lots of food. Everyone had plenty, except the man who had mocked the man of God. As the people stampeded out the gate, this man was trampled to death. Just as Elisha had said, he saw the food but did not eat it.

Because the four lepers did what they could, they saved themselves and the people of Samaria.

Just as the king in the story asked the brothers to build a road to a far away beautiful city, we have been visited by the King of kings, Jesus. He needs us to use our hands and work for His kingdom to help people get to heaven.

> **PLUG-IN** It is time for a staff planning/work session for next *kids POWer hour* series. Save frustration by checking the supply closet and making sure everything needed is on hand. Make this a fun/work time.

Even children can work for the Lord. You decide whether you will have lazy hands or working hands. Just like the four lepers, you can get up and help yourself and others.
Do what you can.

Brainstorm with the children to name things they can do for the kingdom of God. Emphasize that little things, like picking up trash around the church or baby sitting with a little brother or sister so mom or dad can visit the sick, are important. Discuss how these jobs are related to bringing people to Christ.

In I Thessalonians 4:11 we are commanded to "work with [our] own hands." Ask your teacher, your pastor, your parents, what you can do. Jesus has provided us everything we need to get the job done. But we must use our hands to do His work. Just as He strengthened the four crippled men to save the starving people of Samaria, He will strengthen us to help people who need the gospel.

Review

Play a game of Pictionary™. Draw someone using his hands to help in the work of the Lord. Suggestions: a preacher baptizing someone; a mom or dad taking their children to church; a child reading the Bible to an older person; a boy raking the church lawn; a girl cleaning the Sunday school room.

Let the children take turns drawing.

One more Hands-Full Jar drawing before the grand drawing.

Give each child a *POWer house* paper.

Invitation and Prayer (5-? minutes)

Take the paving stones from the wheelbarrow, one at a time, as you teach.
Jesus gave us everything we need to build a road to heaven.
He died for our sins. We die out to sin and self through repentance.
He was buried. We are buried in water in baptism in Jesus' name for the remission of our sins.
He rose again. When we receive the Holy Ghost, we rise to a new life. We know when we receive the Holy Ghost because we speak in a language we did not learn.
Jesus is holy and He wants us to live holy lives.
And He wants us to help others find the way to heaven.
If you have not obeyed the plan of salvation and you want to receive the Holy Ghost—or if you want to dedicate your hands to the Lord to be working hands, come forward. We will pray together.

Have the boys gather on one side of the room and the girls on the other. Then ask them to join hands and pray for one another, as well as themselves.

Unit Three
Character Development

Unit Aim: To help children develop godly qualities in their lives.

Memory Passage: Psalm 134

J = Jesus First
O = Others Second
Y = You Last

Uplifted Hands

13

Scripture Text: Acts 16:16-34; Psalm 63:4, 134:2

 Praise God whatever the circumstances.

 Shop Talk

✓ If an overhead projector is available, make a transparency of the memory passage and the spelling actions. Or write the memory passage on a board and the spelling actions on a poster. Keep the spelling actions in your files. They can be used to spell key words for any lesson—Sunday school, youth services, as well as *kids POWer hour.*

✓ Do you have enough gifts and coins for the joyful handshakes and final drawings?

✓ For the mystery testifier, choose someone who has learned the value of praising God in difficult circumstances. The person should be in place behind the screen before the children enter.

✓ Copy the scripts and the *POWer house* papers.

✓ Choose two older children to do the skit, "Bragger Meets Praiser." Give them a copy several days in advance. Have a practice session.

✓ Put a marker or chalk (depending upon what kind of board you are using) in a compass. Place in Handy Dan's toolbox. Have a short practice of A Lesson from the Toolbox.

✓ With construction paper and rulers, make four flags—red, blue, yellow and green.

✓ Gather items for the prison still scene. Contact people needed to help. This takes planning and preparation, but it is worth the effort. See details under the Illustrated Sermon.

✓ Copy drawings of "senses" from page 124 onto flashcards.

✓ Choose an older child to give Paul's mystery testimony. Give him a copy.

✓ For the review game of charades, write the list of "Praise is . . ." on a poster, board, or transparency. Also write each sentence on a slip of paper for the children to draw.

Schedule

Date: _____

I. POWer of Worship (25-30 minutes)
 A. Welcome (5 minutes)
  • Hands-Full Jars
 B. A Lesson from the Toolbox (5 minutes)
  • *POWer line*
 C. Stand Up for Jesus (4 minutes)
 D. Skit: Bragger Meets Praiser (4 minutes)
 E. Sing unto the Lord (6 minutes)
  • Praise Choruses
  • Dynamo Specials
 F. Lift Up Holy Hands (5 minutes)
  • Praise Report
 G. From Our Hands to Yours (5 minutes)
  • Photo Taking Session
II. POWer of the Word (25-30 minutes)
 A. Action Spelling (6 minutes)
 B. From Hand to Heart (6 minutes)
 C. Illustrated Sermon (12 minutes)
  • Mystery Testimony
  • Prison Still Scene
  • Paul and Silas in Prison
 C. Invitation and Prayer (5-? minutes)
 D. Review
  • Charades: Praise is . . . .

On Hand

- ❏ *kids POWer hour* tape
- ❏ tape player
- ❏ *POWer house* papers
- ❏ Hands-Full Jars, prizes, coins
- ❏ dry erase board and markers or chalkboard and chalk or overhead projector and transparency
- ❏ copies of script and testimony
- ❏ compass
- ❏ mirror
- ❏ mystery testifier screen and spotlight
- ❏ timer
- ❏ camera and film
- ❏ construction paper—red, blue, yellow, green
- ❏ four rulers
- ❏ glue
- ❏ refrigerator box, optional
- ❏ axe
- ❏ paper sword
- ❏ whip
- ❏ drawings of senses
- ❏ brown paper sack
- ❏ black spray paint
- ❏ chain
- ❏ plastic rats and bugs
- ❏ candle
- ❏ biblical robe

POWer of Worship

Welcome (5 minutes)

This is the last *kids POWer hour* for the Hands-Full Jars and the joyful gloves. Why not have enough joyful handshakes that each child gets a prize? Is there a child who is going through a rough time? Give him the kid's glove to wear.

As you welcome guests and acknowledge birthdays, Handy Dan sits at his work bench with his head hidden in his arms. Occasionally his shoulders shake as if he is crying.

A Lesson from the Toolbox (5 minutes)

HANDY DAN, sitting at the work bench, begins to sob dramatically.

DIRECTOR: Puts hand on his shoulder. **Why, Handy Dan, what is the matter?**

DAN: Sobbing and choking. **Don't you know?**

DIRECTOR: **No, I don't. No one has died. You're not sick. You haven't lost your job.**

DAN: Looks up. **In a way I have. I'm so upset I'm not going to be able to sing or pray or praise the Lord.**

DIRECTOR: **Oh, Handy Dan, you shouldn't be like that! We should always praise the Lord.**

DAN: **But I can't. I just can't. Don't you realize this is the last *kids POWer hour* for Handy Dan? I'll be gone and forgotten. No one will even miss me.**

DIRECTOR: **You have been fixing things for us, Handy Dan. It looks like it is time for me to fix something for you. Give me your Bible. I have a prescription for your blues. It's found in I Thessalonians 5:18.** Reads. ***"In every thing give thanks: for this is the will of God in Christ Jesus concerning you."***

DAN: **"In everything give thanks"? That means be thankful that this is my last *kids POWer hour*? I just can't give thanks for that.**

DIRECTOR: **Our *POWer line* today is just for you. Praise God whatever the circumstances.**

DAN: **Praise God whatever the sir-come-where?**

DIRECTOR: **Not "sir-come," but circumstances. Praise God whatever the circumstances.** Pulls a compass out of Handy Dan's toolbox. **What is this, Handy Dan?**

DAN: **It's a compass. You make circles with it.**

DIRECTOR: Makes a circle on a board with the compass. **Does anyone know what the outside of this circle is called? It is a circumference.** Writes both "circumference" and "circumstance" on the board. **These words look alike, don't they? The circumference of a circle is the line that surrounds it. Circumstances are the things that are happening around us.**

Draws a stick figure inside the circle. **Circumstances are things that happen to us or that affect us.** Writes these things around the edge of the circle. **It could be sickness, failing a test, or divorce. Or it could be something wonderful like a friend**

	receiving the Holy Ghost, getting a perfect score on a test, or making a new friend. Whatever the circumstances, we should give thanks and praise God.
DAN:	**Even when it is my last *kids POWer hour*?**
DIRECTOR:	**Yes, but, Brother (real name), this is not your last *kids POWer hour*. This is the last time you will be Handy Dan, but you can still come to *kids POWer hour*.**
DAN:	Sniffs. **I can?**
DIRECTOR:	**Certainly, you can. In fact, next *kids POWer hour*. . . .** Announces plans for the next *kids POWer hour* series.
DAN:	Jumps up and throws hands in the air. **Praise the Lord. I can still come to *kids POWer hour*. That's the best news I've had all day. It's not hard to praise the Lord in those sir-come . . . in those cir-cum-stances.**

PERMISSION TO COPY SCRIPT

Stand Up for Jesus (4 minutes)

The mystery testifier tells of a difficult time in his life which taught him to praise God whatever the circumstance. After the children identify him, give him a round of applause.

Bragger Meets Praiser (4 minutes)

ENTER BRAGGER, a puffed-up boaster. He makes his way to the front, speaking to the children as he comes up the aisle.

BRAGGER:	**Hi! I'm here. Why aren't you standing in my honor? You have surely heard of me. Everyone has! Well, almost everyone. Even if they haven't heard of me, people stand in amazement as I pass by. It's probably my looks.** Takes out a mirror and looks at himself. Smooths his hair and poses like a "muscle man."
	ENTER PRAISER, stands beside Bragger.
PRAISER:	**Hi. What's your name?**
BRAGGER:	**What do you mean? Everybody who is anybody knows my name! What's the most wonderful name you can think of. That's my name.**
PRAISER:	**Jesus is the most wonderful name I know.**
BRAGGER:	**Well, that's not my name. Think of the name of the strongest person you ever heard of. That's my name.**
PRAISER:	**Hummm. Jesus carries everyone's burdens so Jesus is the strongest person I have ever heard of.**
BRAGGER:	**We are getting nowhere. I told you Jesus is not my name. Okay, okay—think of the name of the richest person you have ever heard of. That's my name.**
PRAISER:	**Oh, that's easy. Jesus owns the cattle on a thousand hills. In fact, everything belongs to Him. So Jesus is the name of the richest person.**
BRAGGER:	Exasperated. **That's not my name! Surely you have heard of me. Everyone has! Think of the name of the person who has the biggest, most beautiful house you have ever heard of.**
PRAISER:	Appears to think. **Well, Jesus is the King of kings. His throne is in heaven and the earth is His footstool. He is building mansions He is going to give away. Jesus! That's the name! Praise the name of Jesus!**
BRAGGER:	EXITS, stomping his feet, muttering. **Dumb guy! Doesn't even know my name!**
PRAISER:	**I knew that guy's name all along, didn't you? His name is "Bragger." The Bible says that we should not brag about ourselves. We should brag on Jesus. That's what praising the Lord is—bragging on Him.**
	EXIT PRAISER.

PERMISSION TO COPY SCRIPT

Spelling Actions
A = Stand on right foot
B = Stand on left foot
C = Wave right hand
D = Wave left hand
E = Jump up and down
F = Do a jumping jack
G = Turn in circles
H = Bend right arm at elbow
I = Bend left arm at elbow
J = Point to the ceiling
K = Point at left ear
L = Point at right ear
M = Pull on left ear
N = Pull on right ear
O = Frown
P = Hop on left foot
Q = Hop on right foot
R = Clap hands
S = Yell, "Amen!"
T = Yell, "Hallelujah!"
U = Pat top of head
V = Pat stomach
W = Touch your toes
X = Nod, "Yes"
Y = Shake head, "No"
Z = Curtsy

PERMISSION TO COPY CODE

Time Filler

If there is additional time and the children enjoyed the Action Spelling game, write on slips of paper attributes of Jesus, *e.g.*, way, truth, life, light, love, for them to spell.

Praise God. Everything we need we find in Jesus!

Sing unto the Lord (6 minutes)

"Praise the Name of Jesus"
"Lift Up Your Hands and Praise the Lord"
"Praise Him"
Make this an exciting praise time. Pentecostal worship is alive, and children love it.

Dynamo Special

For the Dynamo Specials ask for volunteers to sing the theme songs learned in this series.

Lift Up Holy Hands (5 minutes)

Devote prayer time to praise reports. Let several children who have praise reports go behind the screen. Send a helper with them to decide when each child testifies. After a child testifies and is identified, he steps from behind the screen, and everyone praises God.

Take prayer requests and lead the children in prayer.

From Our Hands to Yours (5 minutes)

This *POWer hour* should be a celebration of thanksgiving—both to the Lord and the children who have given. If you have divided into teams, give awards to this unit's winners. Give special recognition to the children who worked to earn the money they are giving this *POWer hour*.

Take a picture of the group to send with the offering. If the offering is going for a project in your church, perhaps the total and the children's picture could be printed in the church bulletin or displayed on the bulletin board.

POWer of the Word

Action Spelling (6 minutes)

Post the spelling sheet where all can see (on an overhead is best). Select a student to be the speller and give him the word on a slip of paper. He spells the word in actions. The others guess each letter until the word is spelled out and written on a board.

Psalm 134:2 gives three reasons why we lift our hands in praise: to (1) "bless," (2) "surrender," and (3) "receive."

Example: to spell "bless," the speller would (1) stand on left foot, (2) point at right ear, (3) jump up and down, (4) yell, "Amen!" and (5) yell, "Amen!"

From Hand to Heart (6 minutes)

Use an overhead projector to display Psalm 134 or write it on a board.

Divide the children into four teams by "numbering off," using colors rather than numbers, *e.g.*, red, yellow, blue, green, red, yellow, blue, green. The children need to remember their color.

Ask a helper to time each round, encouraging the children to beat their record.

When the leader holds up a flag (red, yellow, blue, or green), the children with that color quickly stand and shout the first word of the memory passage. The leader holds up another color and those children jump up and shout the second word. The round continues until the whole passage has been said.

For the second round, cover up or erase a few words. For the next round, cover up more words. For the final round turn off the overhead or erase the board.

Review question: **Why do we raise our hands in praise?** to bless, surrender, and receive.

> **PLUG-IN** Do your children understand why we "lift up our hands," "shout with a loud voice," "dance before the Lord," when we worship? Because as we love the Lord with "all our heart, mind, soul, and strength," so we worship Him—not with a part of our being, but all of it.

Worship Chorus (2 minutes)

As the children sing, the person who is going to give Paul's mystery testimony slips behind the screen and puts on a biblical robe.

ILLUSTRATED SERMON

Paul and Silas in Prison (12 minutes)

A copy of this mystery testimony should be given to the one playing the role of Paul.

> I thought I was on God's side,
> But I was only full of pride.
> *Straighten shoulders and push out chest.*
> A light from heaven knocked me down.
> *Falls to knees.*
> I got up blind, from the ground.
> *Gets up and gropes around.*
> That's the day I was changed,
> God my life rearranged.
> *Points up, then to self.*
> Instead of taking saints to jail,
> I was the one who needed bail.
> Even my name was not the same.
> Can you tell me my new name?

> **PLUG-IN** A three-sided refrigerator box could be turned into a prison cell. Chains can be attached to the box wall. Stocks can be made from pieces of cardboard from the part of the box that is cut away so the children can see inside the cell. Add plastic rats and spiders! Perhaps a prisoner has marked off days by etching on the wall? Use your imagination.

PERMISSION TO COPY SCRIPT

After the children guess his name, "Paul" is given a round of applause as he returns to his seat.

While the students watch, create a still scene of a prison cell with chains, a whip, and a whipping post. The cell is empty. The teacher's words and children's imagination will fill it. An adult or helper can be the guard. He has an axe, whip, sword (paper), and wears a black hood (a paper sack spray painted black). The still scene is created while the congregation watches.

Often in the Bible people were thrown into prison. Can you name some?

Begin building the still scene. **Prisons in Bible times were not like prisons today. They were made of stone—cold, damp, dirty stone. Little streams of stagnant-smelling water constantly trickled down the walls, forming pools on the filthy, cold, dirty floors. Insects,** roaches, and lizards, perhaps snakes, large disease-carrying rats with yellow teeth and beady eyes crawled everywhere. There were no restrooms so the sewage mixed with the mud.

Enter the prison guard who takes his position and freezes. **The guards were strong, cruel men who felt no remorse as they tied people to a post and whipped them or beat them with a rod until they were half dead.**

After they were stripped and beaten, prisoners were crammed into these dungeons. Their feet were locked into stocks. The stocks were wooden devices that locked the ankles into a painful position. If the prisoner was left in that position for any time, deep sores erupted because of poor circulation. The prisoners' wrists were cuffed into chains—rusty chains that rubbed and infected the skin.

Prisoners moaned and groaned in agony. Some screamed as they were taken off to the chopping block. The guard laughs menacingly.

Prisons were dark places—no electric lights. At midnight not one ray of light could find its way into the cells, especially the inner prison. It was not a pretty picture.

Let's look in Acts 16 for the story of two preachers who were thrown into a prison that might have been just like the one we have learned about. Show the children how to find Acts 16.

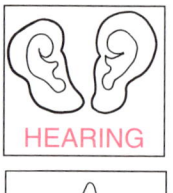

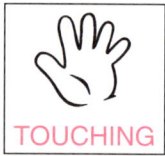

Show the drawings of the five senses. **Humans experience life through the five senses—seeing, smelling, hearing, tasting, and touching.**

Help the children identify with Paul and Silas by imagining what their senses were experiencing in prison. What might they have smelled—sewage? What might they have seen—dying prisoners? What might they have heard—screams of anguish? What might they have tasted—blood from their swollen lips? What might they have touched or been touched by—a rat? Throughout the story, the teacher stops and holds up one of the drawings. The children give input as to what Paul and Silas might have been sensing at that moment.

When I hold up one of these drawings, I want you to tell me what the preachers might have been seeing, hearing, smelling, tasting, or touching.

Paul and Silas had gone to Thyatira to preach. On their way to a prayer meeting, they were followed by a girl possessed by an evil spirit. Through the spirit of fortune telling, this girl made a lot of money for her masters. She followed Paul and Silas and cried, "These men are the servants of the most high God, which show us the way of salvation." Even though what she said was true, her life made a mockery of the things of God.

Paul was grieved by her spirit and cast the demon out of her. That caused her masters to lose their source of income, so they falsely accused Paul and Silas. The citizens of the city rose up against God's men. The officials had Paul and Silas beaten—many, many stripes were laid on their backs. Then they were thrown into prison. The guard laughs ominously again.

The guard took charge of the prisoners. He put them in the inner prison. Hold up drawing of nose and let the children respond. **Imagine the smell of sewage and death.**

He chained their wrists to the wall of the prison. Hold up the drawing of the hand. What were Paul and Silas feeling? **No doubt, they felt great pain as their arms were stretched and their wrists were shackled by rusty chains.**

He locked their ankles into stocks. Hold up the drawing of the mouth. **Paul and Silas may have tasted blood in their mouths from the beating.**

The guard slammed the heavy door and left. Hold up the drawing of the ear. **Paul and Silas probably heard fellow prisoners moaning and groaning, even cursing.**

God's men were in the dark—total darkness! Hold up drawing of the eye. **They could not see anything!**

Hold up drawing of the hand. **But they probably could feel the rats and roaches as they scampered over them. And they could feel the terrible painful throbbing of their wounds and the pins-and-needles sensation in their arms and legs.**

What would you do in this situation? Let children respond.

Do you know what Paul and Silas did? They began to brag on Jesus! They praised the Lord! It was midnight! It was dark, smelly, and scary. But that did not stop them from praising the Lord. Some scholars think they sang praises from the Psalms. They may have sung something like the chorus we sing from Psalm 118:24. Lead the children in singing, "This Is the Day that the Lord Hath Made." **Or they might have sung a chorus like the one we sing from Psalm 113:3.** Lead the children in singing, "From the Rising of the Sun."

Paul and Silas were believers in our *POWer line*.
Praise God whatever the circumstances.

When they bragged on Jesus, even though they were in prison and experiencing horrible things, they got His attention.

There was a great earthquake and the shackles fell off. The walls shook; the prison doors opened. The prisoners could have escaped, but they did not.

The guard took out his sword to kill himself. He thought the prisoners had escaped! But Paul cried out, "Do thyself no harm. We are all here."

GUARD: Rips off his hood. **Bring me a light!**

Hand him a candle. **Trembling, the guard fell down before Paul and Silas and asked:**

GUARD: **Sirs, what must I do to be saved?**

They told him to believe on the Lord Jesus Christ and they preached to him. We know the guard repented because he took Paul and Silas home with him, washed their backs, and fed them. That night the guard was baptized. Truly believing in the Lord Jesus always causes a person to obey God's Word.

Because Paul and Silas bragged on Jesus, even during a horrible time, the guard and his family were saved—and Paul and Silas were delivered.

Praise God!

Invitation and Prayer (5-? minutes)

As the musician plays softly, refer back to the illustration of "circumstances."

At some time everyone experiences bad times. Perhaps there are some unpleasant circumstances in your life right now. Add to the illustrations things which you know or feel that your children are experiencing, *e.g.*, rejection, abuse, failure, poverty, sickness. **It is not easy to "praise God" in some circumstances. It is easier to grumble and mumble and worry and fret than it is to shout and sing.**

But remember, no matter what the circumstances in our lives, victory comes when we have a right attitude. When you brag on Jesus, you get His attention. And He can change your circumstances.

Let's bow our heads and close our eyes. If you have a need you want Jesus to meet—perhaps you need the Holy Ghost, or healing, or help with a problem—get His attention right now. Raise your hands and start praising Him.

The Handy Helpers should move around the room, praying with the children.

Review

Have a game of charades. Display the "Praise is . . ." sentences on a board, poster, or transparency.

Praise is . . .
- like eagle's wings that let you soar above troubles.
- like a rocking chair to aching bones.
- like a warm blanket on a cold night.
- like ropes around a lion's mouth.
- like gasoline in a car.
- like the key to a treasure chest.
- like a cool breeze on a summer day.
- like an elevator into heaven's throne room.
- like a bridge over a deep ravine.
- like a sign that points the way out of a dark, damp cave.
- like a candle in the night.
- like Ben-Gay™ or Icy-Hot™ for the heart muscle.
- like an anchor in a raging sea.
- like focusing after getting badly needed glasses.
- like hip boots in knee-deep mud.

The first player draws a slip of paper containing a sentence. Allow a specific time for each act. At the end of the time or when the children guess, erase or mark that sentence off. The next player draws another sentence.

When we brag on Jesus, we receive comfort and deliverance.

Have the final Hands-Full Jars drawings.

Give each child a *POWer house* paper as he leaves. Remind all to bring a friend to *kids POWer hour* next time as an exciting new series will begin.

Two Great Commandments

The first of all the commandments is,
Hear, O Israel;
The Lord our God is one Lord:
And thou shalt love the Lord thy God
With all thy heart,
And with all thy soul,
And with all thy mind,
And with all thy strength:
This is the first commandment.
This is the first command.

And the second is like,
Namely this,
Thou shalt love thy neighbor as thyself.
There is none other commandment
Greater than these.

by Pam Eddings

J-O-Y-F-U-L H-A-N-D-S

Tune: M-I-C-K-E-Y M-O-U-S-E

J-O-Y-F-U-L H-A-N-D-S!
Joyful hands, joyful hands
Together let us raise our hands
up high, High! HIGH! HIGH!
Come along and sing this song
and join the jubilee.
J-O-Y-F-U-L H-A-N-D-S!

by Paula Townsley

Stand Right Up for Jesus

by Pamela J. Taylor

stand right up for Je - sus I have no doubt— I'm gonna
can! I'll plant my feet and fear no heat 'cause
Je - sus holds my hand!

Transparency master   PERMISSION TO COPY

My J-O-Yful Hands

How can my hands please Jesus
and make Him number one?
I'll worship Him and do my best
to hear Him say "Well done."

How can my hands bless others
who hurt and lose their way?
I'll help and reach and do my part
Every-day when I pray.

How can my hands help myself
To be what I should be?
Holding hands with Jesus,
Always working, serving faithfully.

chorus
J-O-Yful hands, J-O-Yful hands,
Jesus, Others, and You;
J-O-Yful hands, J-O-Yful hands,
To accomplish all God said to do.
Together there's nothing we can't do.

by Pam Eddings and Suzanne Priddy

Behold, Bless Ye the Lord

Behold, bless ye the LORD,
All ye servants of the LORD,
Which by night stand
In the house of the LORD,
Lift up your hands in the sanctuary,
And bless the LORD.

by Pam Eddings

God Loves the Truth

God loves the truth—
He hates a lie;
His Word tells us so;
I'll tell the truth;
I will not lie
No matter where I go!

by Pamela J. Taylor and Suzanne Priddy

Transparency master PERMISSION TO COPY

Love the Lord

Tune: London Bridge

Place hand over heart.

Love the Lord with your heart and soul,
With your heart and soul,
with your heart and soul.
Love the Lord with heart and soul.
And make Him number one.

Point to temple.

Love the Lord with all your mind,
All your mind, all your mind.
Love the Lord with all your mind.
And make Him number one.

Flex muscles.

Love the Lord with all your strength,
All your strength,
all your strength.
Love the Lord with
all your strength.
And make Him number one.

by Paula Townsley and Suzanne Priddy

MARK 12:29-30

And Jesus answered him, The first of all the commandments is, Hear, O Israel; The Lord our God is one Lord: And thou shalt love the Lord thy God with all thy heart, and with all thy soul, and with all thy mind, and with all thy strength: this is the first commandment.

Transparency master PERMISSION TO COPY

MARK 12:31

And the second is like, namely this, Thou shalt love thy neighbor as thyself. There is none other commandment greater than these.

Behold, bless ye the LORD, all ye servants of the LORD, which by night stand in the house of the LORD. Lift up your hands in the sanctuary, and bless the LORD. The LORD that made heaven and earth bless thee out of Zion.

Psalm 134

Transparency master PERMISSION TO COPY

At God's House

We talked about walking hand in hand with Jesus. Anyone—moms, dads, grandparents, boys, girls—can walk hand in hand with Jesus by obeying His Word.

➡ Draw lines to match the gloves.

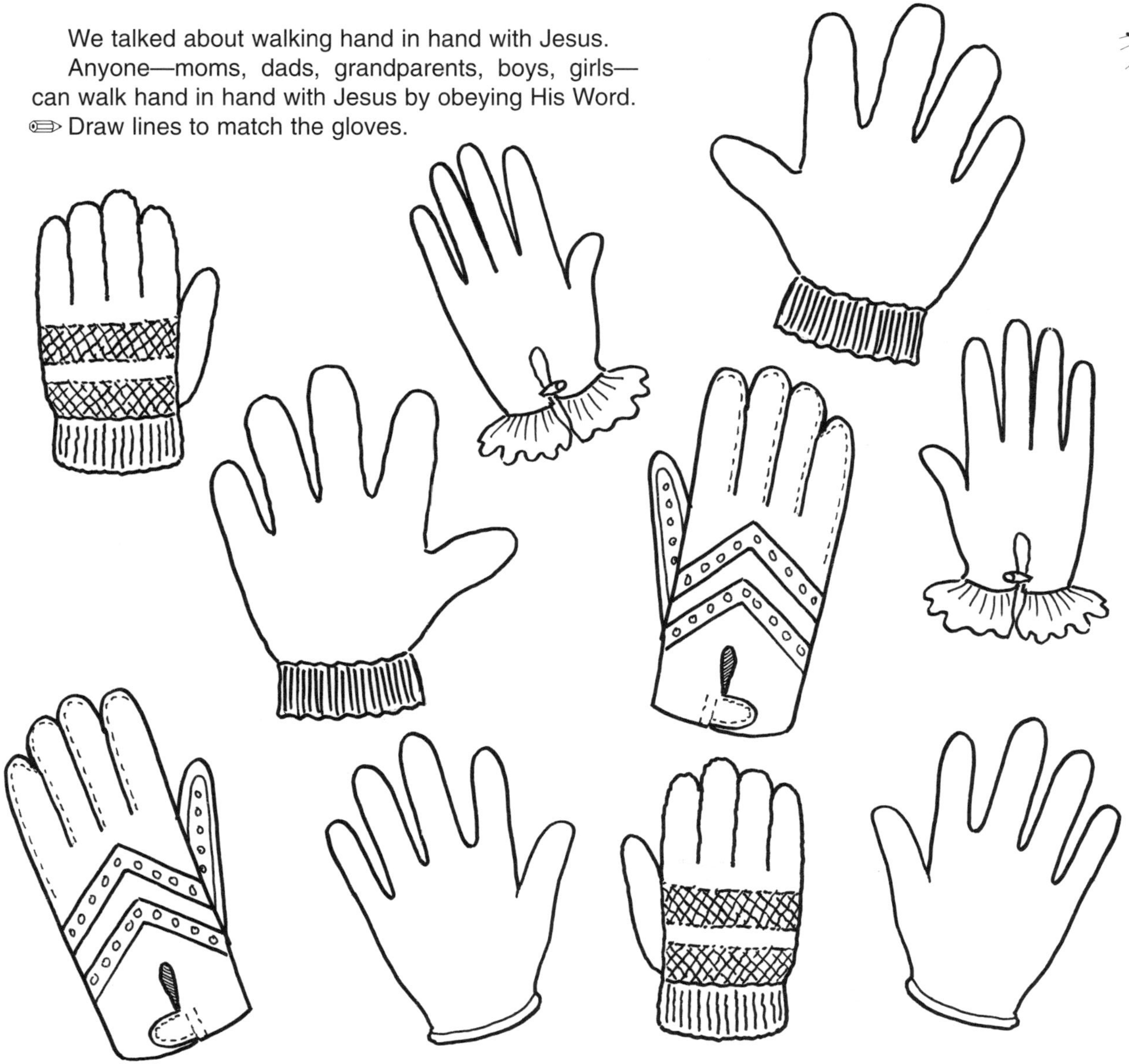

At Your House

✶ Walking hand in hand with Jesus pays more than it costs.

Mark 12:29-30
And Jesus answered him, The first of all the commandments is, Hear, O Israel; The Lord our God is one Lord:

Dear Parent,

In kids POWer hour we started a new series, "J-O-Yful Hands." We will be stressing a formula for individual joy:

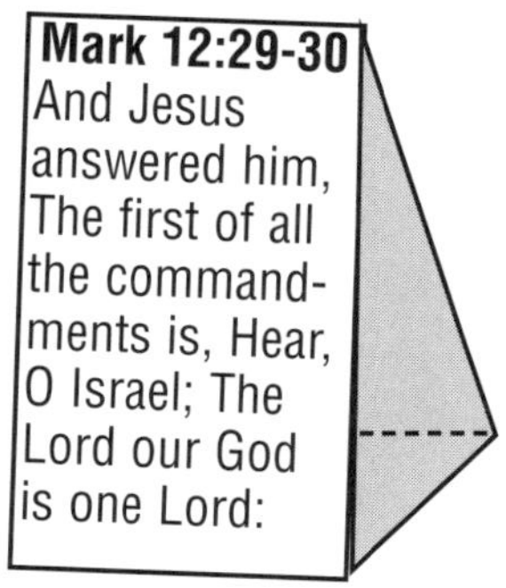

Jesus First,

Others Second,

You (your child) Last.

Today we talked about walking hand in hand with Jesus. We learned that to do this we must let Him be the boss. He gives the orders—leads the way.

✓ *Do a role play. Pretend that you are the child and your child is Jesus. Join hands and walk around the house or outside, letting the child lead the way. Point out pretend places, such as, the church, the liquor store, the nursing home, school. Ask: Would Jesus take us there? Can you walk with Jesus and go here?*

✓ *Memorize it. Our memory passage for this unit is Mark 12:29-30. It's rather lengthy and your preschooler will need help. Write it on a stand-up sign—a piece of posterboard folded into three segments, as illustrated. Place on the table. At each meal let the preschooler turn the sign, while the rest of the family reads the verse.*

kids POWer hour staff

At God's House

From the crossword puzzle, find the words to fill in the blanks which tell some exciting things that happened to Peter because he decided to follow Jesus.

```
D
E   W A T E R
A N G E L
D   T
  M E N
  O
  U
  T
  H
```

He caught a fish with a coin in its _____.

He raised Dorcas from the _____.

An _____ freed him from prison.

He fished for _____, instead of fish.

He walked on _____.

He healed the lame man at the _____ Beautiful.

He baptized Cornelius' household in water in Jesus' _____.

Powerhouse 1

Wow! Following Jesus is exciting!

Walking hand in hand with Jesus pays more than it costs.

Peter became Jesus' right hand man. You can be someone's "right hand." You do know that means to be their "helper," don't you? We say "right hand" because most people use their right hand to do their work.

By the way, the Bible tells about some special guys who were left-handed. Read about them in Judges 20:16.

Fill in the blanks in this hand. Cut it out and give it to someone you will help one day this week. You will be surprised at the rewards which come to "right hands."

MEMO
TO: _____
I will be your right hand on _____
FROM: _____

At Your House

At God's House

We learned three of the most powerful words in the world. Trace the dotted lines to spell these words.

✏️ Color the pop-up card. Sign your name. ✂️ Cut on the dotted line, fold on solid lines, and give it to someone you love.

At Your House

When we love Jesus, we worship with our hearts and serve with our hands.

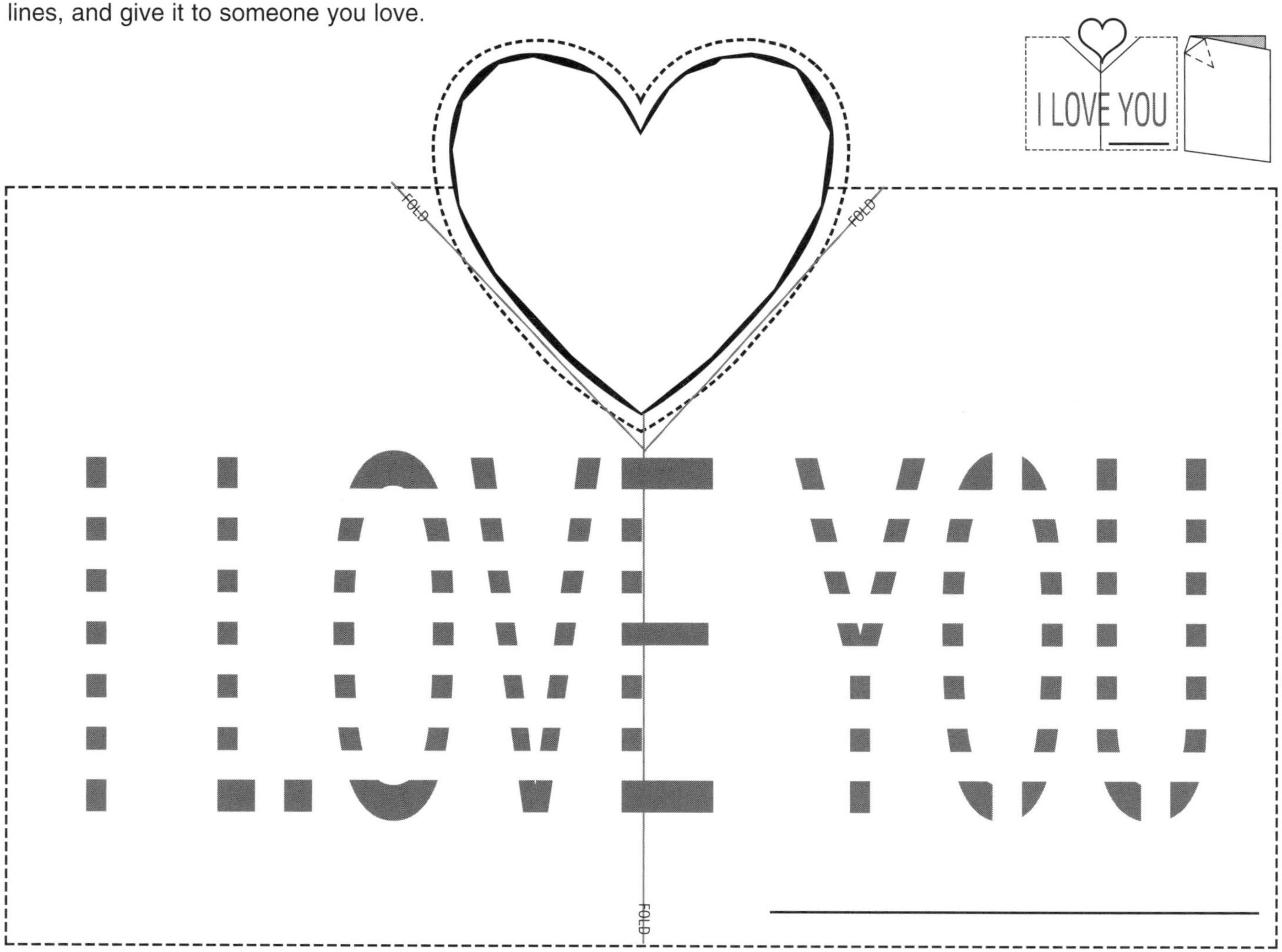

Dear Parent,

At kids POWer hour our lesson title was *"Heart in Hand."* We learned how we express the love in our hearts by what we do with our hands.

Here are some suggestions on how you can help your child apply this principle to daily life.

- **Give your child a job to do for you.** When he does it, give him a big bear hug and say, "I'm so glad you love me enough to do <u>so-and-so</u>." Make a direct connection between love and service.

- **Write "love notes"** to your child. Put one on his pillow, or in his pocket, or wherever. Those notes can be life-long memory makers.

We love your child and we want to serve him and your family.

kids POWer hour staff

I LOVE YOU

take home paper ages 7-11

At God's House

Mark 12:30 tells us to love the Lord with four things. Unscramble these words. Then connect them with the matching symbol.

ndim _____

luso _____

htgnerts _____

anthe _____

Powerhouse 2

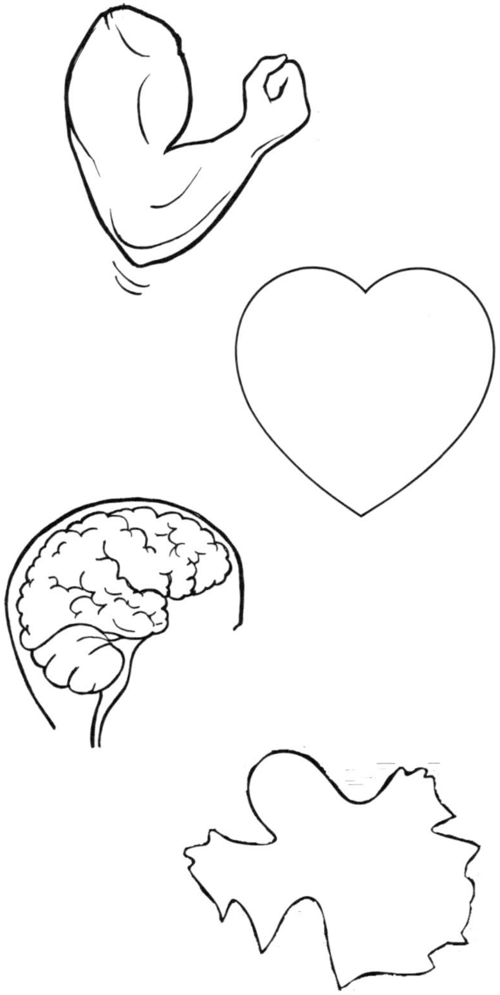

When we love Jesus, we worship with our hearts and serve with our hands.

Write a note on this pop-up card to someone you love. Be sure to include those three powerful words, "I love you." Color it. ✂ Then cut it out on the dotted lines. Fold it. Place it in a "surprise" place where the one you are writing to will find it.

At Your House

Permission to photocopy this page granted for church use.

At God's House

✏️ Color and ✂️ cut out these finger puppets of the widow and a rich man. Use them to tell the story of the widow's mites to your parents or friends.

At Your House

✝️ **When we give all, it is much.**

Dear Parent,

We learned at kids POWer hour that God does not count what we give, but what we have left. He is much more interested in how we give than how much we give.

■ *Ask each family member to save their change for a month. Then go shopping. Buy stamps, soap, shampoo, etc. Include an unsigned friendship card. Arrange in a basket and take to an elderly person.*

Set your gift on the porch, ring the bell, and leave quietly. This project is guaranteed to put your family on such a high that you will not come down for days.

— kids POWer hour staff

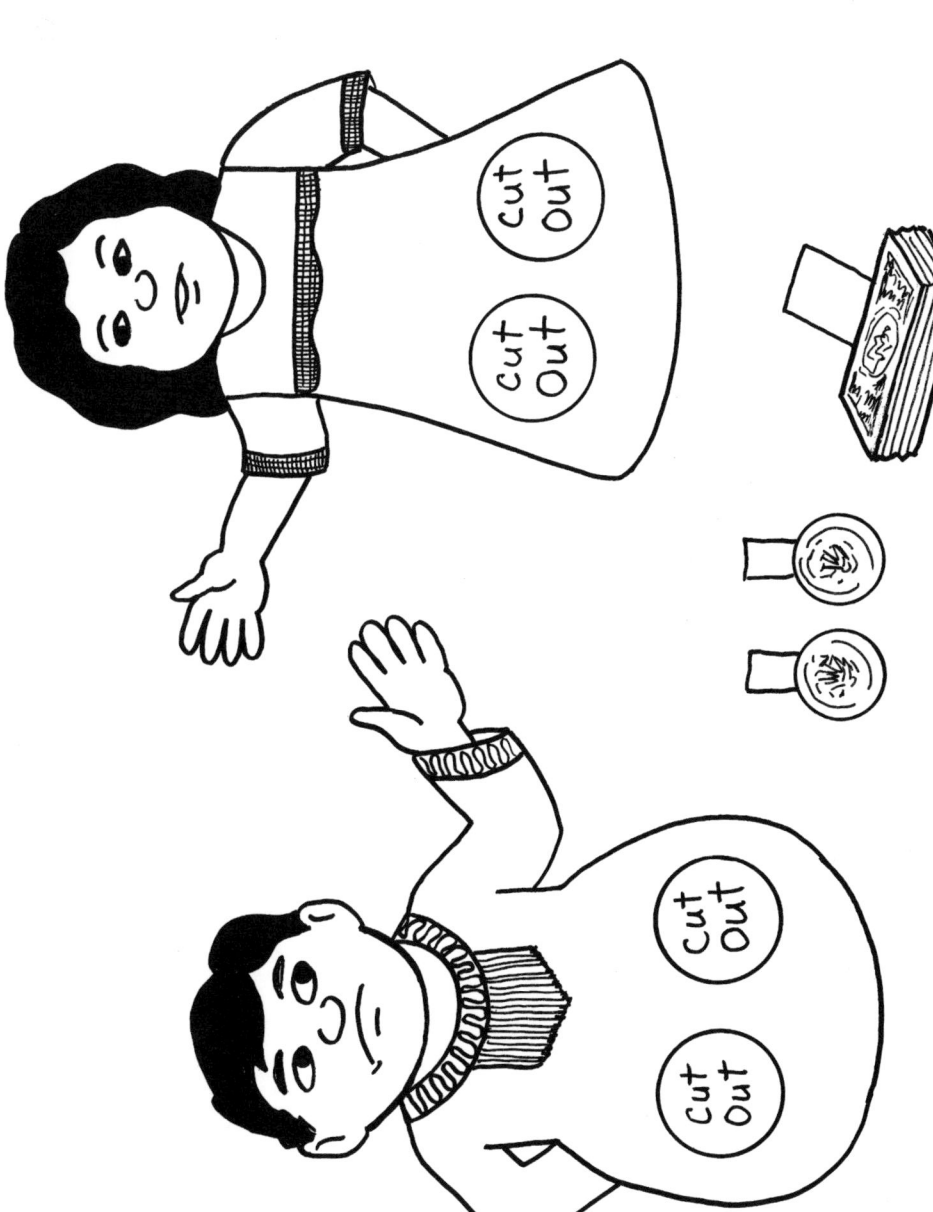

At God's House

To find what God loves cross out all the letters that are in **NOBODY**.

A	B	C	D	H	E	O
E	N	O	R	D	Y	F
U	B	D	L	G	I	Y
N	D	V	E	O	R	D

God loves __ __ __ __ __ __ __ __ __ .

Powerhouse B

When we give all, it is much.

Ask your parents if your family can do something secretly for an elderly friend.
Ask each family member to save their change for a month. Then go shopping. Buy stamps, soap, shampoo, etc. Include an unsigned friendship card. Arrange in a basket and take to your friend.
Set your gift on the porch, ring the bell, and quietly leave. You will bless them and also yourselves.

Fill in the missing vowels to find what you will learn from a project like this.

_ t _ s   m _ r _   bl _ ss _ d   t _
g _ v _   th _ n   t _   r _ c _ _ v _ .

The answer can be found in Acts 20:35.

God does not count what we give, but what we have left.

He is much more interested in how we give than how much we give.

At Your House

take home paper ages 4-6

At God's House

People who cannot hear often talk with their hands. You can learn to use your hands to spell "Jesus." Here's how you do it.

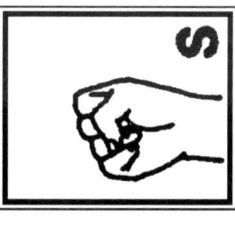
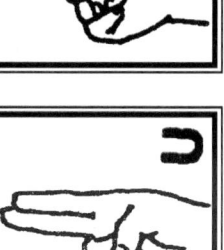
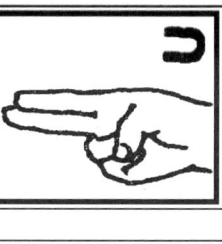
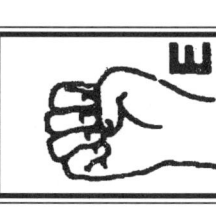
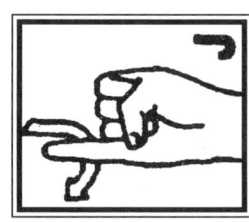

👉 Color your Dynamo friends, who are happy to know Jesus.

Permission to photocopy this page granted for church use.

At Your House

✝ **Jesus is always with us. We can talk to Him any time.**

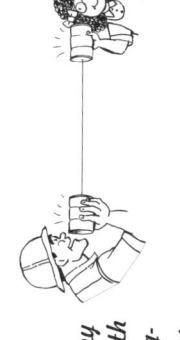

Dear Parent,

Jesus met two of His followers on the road to Emmaus. They walked and talked with Him but did not recognize Him. Wonder how many times we do the same thing?

At kids POWer hour today we talked about communicating with God. We learned that prayer is both talking and listening. We also learned that God can talk to us in our hearts and through His Word. Would you help reinforce what your child learned today? Here are some suggestions.

■ Teach your child to listen to the preaching of God's Word by giving him simple listening assignments. "Every time the preacher says, 'Jesus,' make a mark on a piece of paper. We will count it when we get home." Or "Every time the preacher says 'love' (or some other key word), you can squeeze my hand." Or "Count with your fingers the number of times the preacher reads from the Bible."

■ Take your child outside and listen for sixty seconds. Then talk about what you heard.

■ Add a short fifteen-second listening time to the end of your nightly prayer. You might be surprised to hear what God has to tell you, as well as your child.

kids POWer hour *staff*

At God's House

Sometimes communication must be sent secretly—especially when one is in danger. Prayer can be sent to God even without saying a word! God knows our thoughts. If you ever need to talk with God secretly, like before a test at school, "think" a prayer!

Soldiers learn Morse Code—a system of long and short beeps to spell out messages. Ships also use the same system with flashes of light. Use the Morse Code to decode this message.

A .-	F ..-.	K -.-	P .--.	U ..-
B -...	G --.	L .-..	Q --.-	V ...-	Z --..
C -.-.	H	M --	R .-.	W .--	& .-...
D -..	I ..	N -.	S ...	X -..-	
E .	J .---	O ---	T -	Y -.--	

-- . ...
.--. .-. .- -.--
. ...- . .-. -.--
-.. .- -.--

Jesus is always with us. We can talk to Him any time.

At Your House

↳ In Morse code write a note to a friend inviting them to church. They will have fun decoding the message, and you will be communicating with them about God.

A .-	F ..-.	K -.-	P .--.	U ..-
B -...	G --.	L .-..	Q --.-	V ...-	Z --..
C -.-.	H	M --	R .-.	W .--	& .-...
D -..	I ..	N -.	S ...	X -..-	
E .	J .---	O ---	T -	Y -.--	

At God's House

POWerhouse 5

At Your House

✝ **True joy comes when we put Jesus and others before self.**

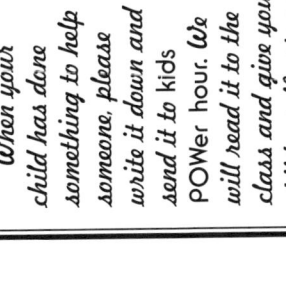

Dear Parent,

During the next five weeks we will be discussing our ability to help others.

When your child has done something to help someone, please write it down and send it to kids POWer hour. We will read it to the class and give your child a self-esteem booster.

✓ Try this. Take your family and help at a food pantry or shelter. Nothing works better than the example of a respected adult.

Thanks for helping to reinforce what we learned at God's house.

kids POWer hour staff

One little, two little, three little fingers,
Four little, five little, six little fingers,
Seven little, eight little, nine little fingers,
Ten little helping fingers.

Ten Little Helping Fingers
Tune: Ten Little Indians

✂ Cut out these hands and use the fingers to sing a new song. When you finish, use the hands to clap for yourself.

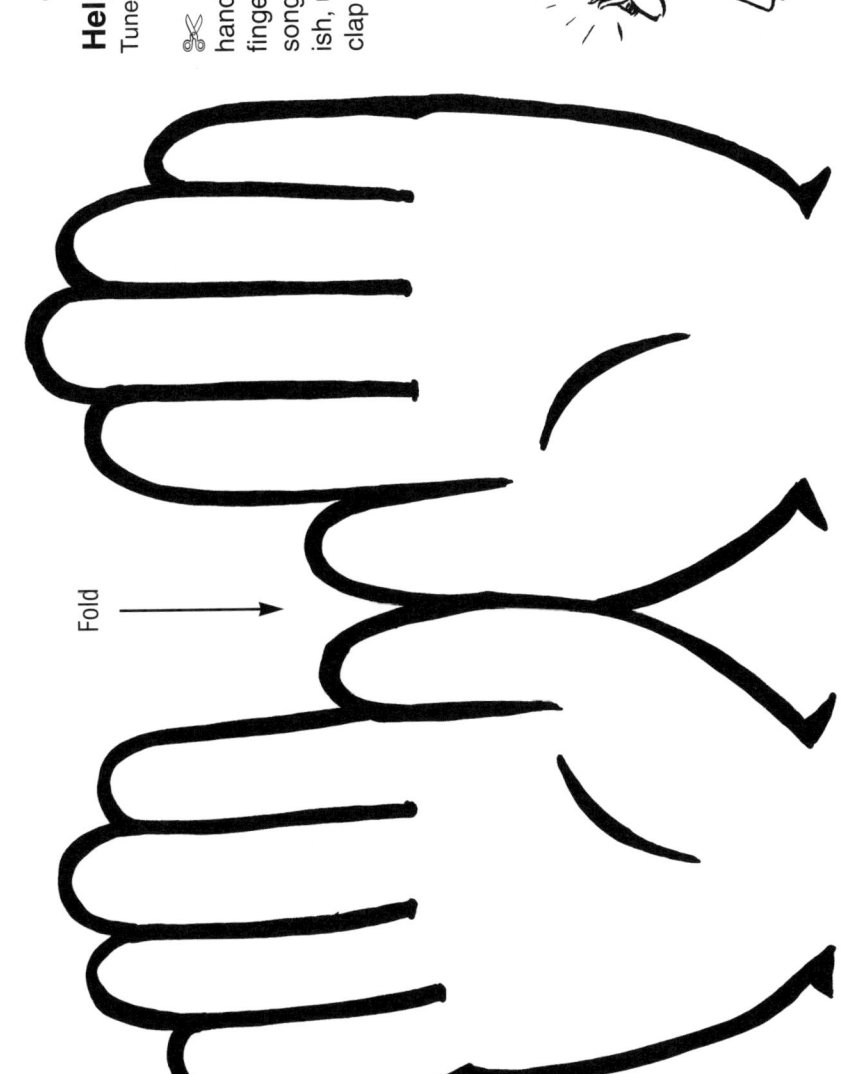

Fold →

At God's House ——  —— At Your House

Helping Hands Coupons

True joy comes when we put Jesus and others before self.

Dear Parent:
During this week I will help by doing the following jobs. Use the coupons as you need them.

Love,
_____

GOOD FOR
ONE TIME
WATCHING LITTLE BROTHER OR SISTER so you can have time alone.

GOOD FOR
ONE TIME
TAKING OUT THE TRASH

GOOD FOR
ONE JOB
YOUR CHOICE

GOOD FOR
ONE JOB
YOUR CHOICE

GOOD FOR
ONE
TABLE CLEANING

GOOD FOR
ONE EXTRA BED MAKING
(means any bed not mine)

GOOD FOR
ONE
PUTTING AWAY THE LAUNDRY

At God's House

POWerhouse

These children are from different races or cultures. Color them.

We should reach out to others, no matter what their race.

At Your House

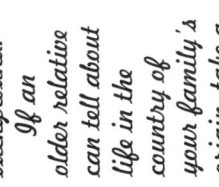
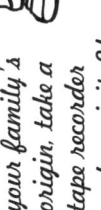

Dear Parent,

This week we discussed diverse cultures. Talk to your children about their ethnic background. If an older relative can tell about life in the country of your family's origin, take a tape recorder and go visit. You will never regret getting on tape your family's history. Involve your children in this project.

Understanding our differences makes us more tolerant of others' differences.

kids POWer hour staff

take home paper ages 7-11

At God's House ___

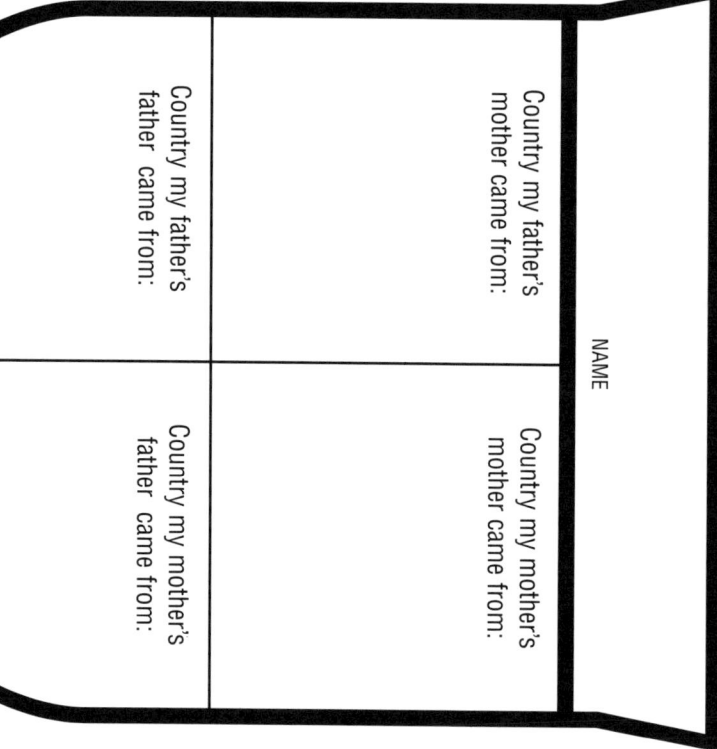

We should reach out to others, no matter what their race.

At Your House ___

Do you know your cultural background? Fill out this coat of arms to give a picture of your heritage.

NAME	
Country my father's mother came from:	Country my mother's mother came from:
Country my father's father came from:	Country my mother's father came from:

Talk to your parents and/or grandparents about their ethnic background. If an older relative can tell about life in the country of your family's origin, take a tape recorder and go visit. You will never regret getting your family's history on tape.

Understanding our **DIFFERENCES** makes us more tolerant of others' **DIFFERENCES**.

Here are some sample questions you might ask.

▷ Tell me about your life as a child in (country).
▷ What games did you play as a child?
▷ What holidays are special in that country?
▷ Why did you (or your parents) come to this country?
▷ How was family life in (country) different from family life here?
▷ What were your favorite foods?
▷ Describe a church service in (country).

Permission to photocopy this page granted for church use.

At God's House

7

At Your House

My neighbor is anyone who needs me.

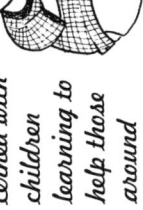

Dear Parent,

This week we are concerned with children learning to help those around them.

If you and your child could do something to help a neighbor, it would reinforce this concept. It might be feeding or caring for a pet, picking up some groceries at the store, putting their newspaper on the porch, helping in the yard, etc.

Remind your child to tell us at kids POWer hour about your family's project.

kids POWer hour staff

✏️ Color and ✂️ cut out this note and put it on a neighbor's door. Be sure to watch for their answer.

We want to help

Is there anything we can do for you?

If so, please make a note of it on the back of this card and tape it to your door. We'll be watching for it.

From Your Neighbors,

_____

take home paper ages 7-11

At God's House

Powerhouse 7

My neighbor is anyone who needs me.

At Your House

Can you find these words from today's Bible story in this word search?

GOOD SAMARITAN PRIEST
ROBBERS NEIGHBOR LEVITE
WOUNDED INNKEEPER
JEW DONKEY

N	G	J	D	E	D	N	U	O	W
E	R	O	K	B	O	C	W	N	D
I	P	E	O	D	F	E	A	R	S
G	R	A	P	D	J	T	P	A	R
H	I	M	X	E	I	L	G	N	E
B	E	P	M	R	E	S	S	Z	B
O	S	R	A	M	Y	K	E	M	I
R	T	M	L	F	S	K	N	H	O
L	A	E	T	I	V	E	L	N	R
S	D	O	N	K	E	Y	G	Y	I

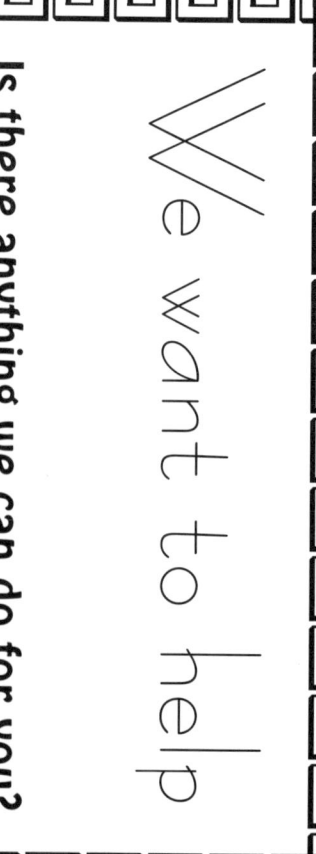

We want to help

Is there anything we can do for you?

If so, please make a note of it on the back of this card and tape it to your door. We'll be watching for it.

From Your Neighbors,
_____

This week we are concerned with helping those around us. Use this card to reach out and help a neighbor.

Permission to photocopy this page granted for church use.

At God's House

😞 Draw a sad face in the circle if the picture would make someone feel bad.

☺ Draw a happy face if it would make them feel good.

✏ Color the picture.

At Your House

✝ We can help those who are disabled.

Dear Parent,

Our focus at kids POWer hour today was on helping someone who is unable to help themselves.

Does your family have a physically challenged friend? If so, take your child to visit them. Or perhaps you have an elderly relative who is in a nursing home. Help your child become comfortable around those who are disabled.

✓ *Try this. Make a tape of your family devotions and take to a disabled or elderly friend. Add lots of singing. Music is not necessary. Your friend will love hearing your child sing. And your child will love making the tape.*

kids POWer hour staff

take home paper ages 7-11

At God's House

At Your House

✂ Fill out this card. ✂ Cut it out, then fold on the dotted lines so that "You are SPECIAL" is on the outside. Put it in an envelope and mail it to a friend who is physically challenged.

We can help those who are disabled.

You Are SPECIAL

I Like You Because

_____
_____
_____
_____
_____
_____
_____
_____
love,
_____

Permission to photocopy this page granted for church use.

At Your House

 Children can help the pastor.

Dear Parent,

Our emphasis today is pastor appreciation. Many churches have pastor appreciation in October, but often the children are not part of the program.

This POWer hour's activities gave your child an outlet to express his appreciation for the man of God.

You could enhance this concept by allowing your child to make a gift for the pastor (even a hand-drawn picture will do) to accompany this "Thank You" card.

Thanks for working with us to instill in your child a love for the man of God.

kids POWer hour staff

At God's House

WANTED by everyone

a Pastor like ours.

Thank you for being such a good pastor.

Love, _____

take home paper ages 7-11

At God's House

✂ Cut out this card. Fold on the dotted lines. On the inside, write a verse thanking your pastor for what he does for you.

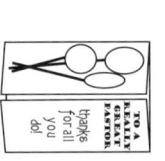

At Your House

✂ Children can help the pastor.

TO A REALLY GREAT PASTOR

thanks for all you do!

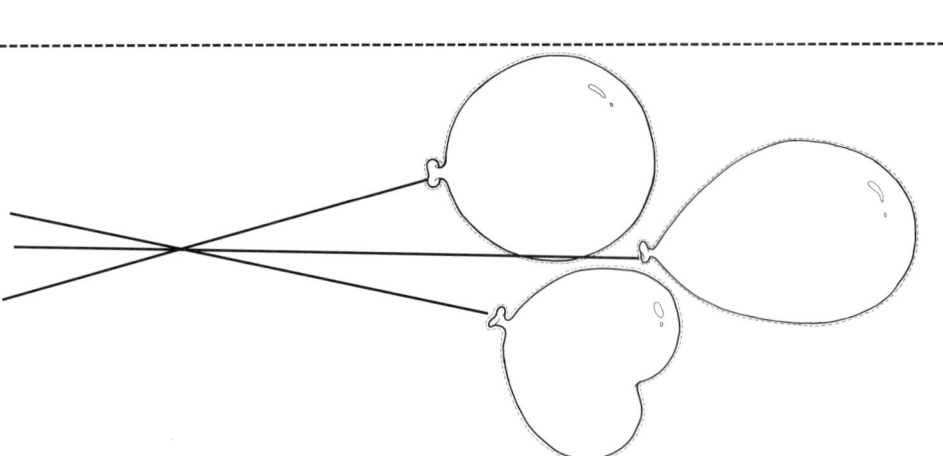

At home make a craft to give the pastor along with this card. Ask your parents for suggestions.

Permission to photocopy this page granted for church use.

kids POWer hour 10

At God's House

At Your House

Stand firm for right.

Dear Parent,

At kids POWer hour we talked about standing firm against negative peer pressure.

Sometimes it is just "God and me," as it was with Daniel when he was thrown in the lions' den. Sometimes others stand with us, as in the case of the three Hebrew children. Whatever the number, when we stand for right, God is with us and that's enough.

Children often pressure parents to "go along with the crowd" because "everybody else is doing it." If you are currently involved in such a situation, talk to your child about why you are taking the stand you are taking. "Just because" is not a good answer. Often when children understand why you are doing what you are doing, the argument ceases and lifelong convictions are formed.

✓ Try this. During family devotions go through magazines and newspapers looking for pictures and stories of people who are standing for right. Discuss what is happening. Send this article to the next kids POWer hour with your child so he can receive a bonus hand print.

Some day your child will rise up and call you "blessed" for standing for right.

kids POWer hour staff

Can you say 'no' to sin?

Yes, because Jesus helps me.

👉 Use a black marker to trace over the lines. What word did you spell? Color the sign.

take home paper ages 4-6

Permission to photocopy this page granted for church use.

take home paper ages 7-11

At God's House

Sometimes it helps us better understand a Bible verse when we say it in our words. Match the phrases from Psalm 134 to the ones worded as we might say them.

"Behold,

bless ye the LORD,

all ye servants of the LORD, which by night stand in the house of the LORD.

Lift up your hands in the sanctuary, and bless the LORD. The LORD that made heaven and earth

bless thee

out of Zion."

You kneel down and love and honor God by praising the LORD,

all you worshipers of the LORD which by night stand in the house of the LORD.

Look here and see!

You kneel down and love and honor God by praising the LORD,

out of God's special place.

Lift up your hands in the church and kneel down and love and honor God by praising the LORD—the LORD that made heaven and earth.

Powerhouse 10

Stand firm for right.

Look through newspapers and magazines for stories or pictures of people taking a stand for right. Bring that to the next kids POWer hour to receive a hand print in a Special Projects Jar for a drawing.

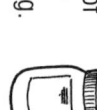

At Your House

If someone tried to get you to read a dirty magazine, what would you tell them?

Permission to photocopy this page granted for church use.

POWerhouse 11

At God's House

Micaiah was happy because he told the truth.

Make a happy face on Micaiah by gluing yarn on for a smile. Stick a band-aid on his thumb.

At Your House

Be honest whatever the cost.

Dear Parent,

At kids POWer hour we learned that there is no such thing as a "little white fib." A fib is a lie, and a lie is a lie. We also learned that it pays to be honest, even when it costs us.

Ask your child to tell you about the band-aid on his thumb.

Here is a good lesson for family devotions to help your child understand the seriousness of lying.

✓ Try it. Collect six building blocks. Wrap five in yellow paper and let your child draw a happy face on each. Wrap the sixth block in white paper and draw a sad face on it.

Begin building a structure as you talk about building our lives on God's Word. Put three yellow, happy face blocks in a row. Build the second level with one happy face and one sad. Sometimes a little white lie seems harmless, even helpful. Finally, put the last yellow, happy face block on the third tier. The structure looks well-built, but it is not because one lie is built in. Remove the white block and the structure will fall.

Talk about repentance. Rewrap the white block with yellow paper. Draw a happy face on it and rebuild.

— kids POWer hour staff

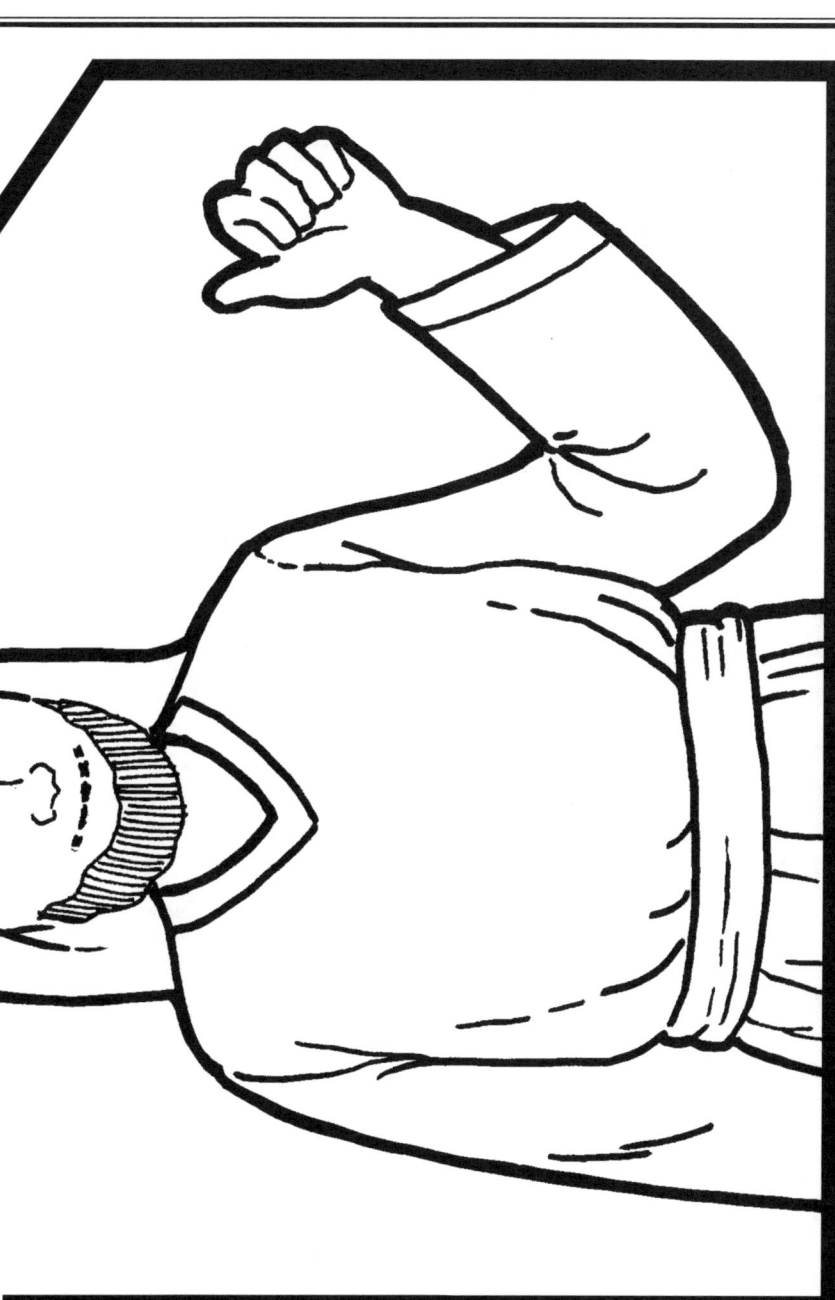

take home paper ages 7-11

At God's House

Micaiah found that telling the truth can be painful. Sometimes we must suffer for being honest. We can be sure, though, that God will reward those who are truthful.

Find the words of Revelation 22:15 that describe those who will NOT be found in heaven, in the word search below ("and" is only used once in the puzzle). (The "dogs" named here are not four-legged animals, but people who live immoral, ungodly lives.)

S	O	R	C	E	R	E	R	S	O	H	S
A	Y	T	U	O	H	T	I	W	T	R	Q
K	N	R	R	Q	X	O	M	E	E	R	W
N	I	D	O	S	G	E	V	G	K	E	S
F	G	D	Z	F	R	O	N	Z	B	V	R
G	J	C	O	A	L	O	W	C	K	E	E
W	V	V	K	L	M	G	F	W	O	R	W
N	P	K	S	E	A	R	P	W	R	S	E
N	N	G	R	W	A	T	E	U	K	O	D
G	O	O	T	Z	R	Z	E	I	H	R	W
D	H	E	E	B	O	A	H	R	L	W	U
W	Q	A	H	T	E	K	A	M	S	A	M

 11

Play a word game with your best friend at school. At random times throughout the day, say, "I will. . . ." The friend is to respond, "tell the truth." Switch lines from time to time by saying, "Tell the truth," to which the response is, "I will."

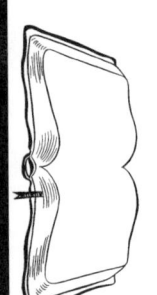

✈ **Be honest whatever the cost.**

Pray that God will help you be strong enough to always tell the truth, even if it causes you pain. Ask for forgiveness for any lies you have told. God wants to forgive you.

At Your House

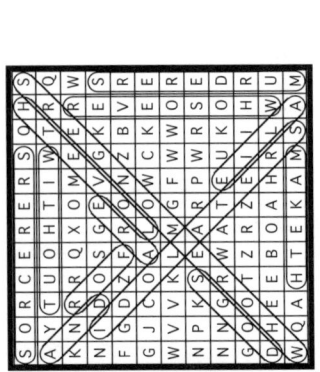

Permission to photocopy this page granted for church use.

At God's House

We should do what we can with our hands.
👉 These people are working with their hands. Match the person with the tool that he or she is using.

POWer house 12

At Your House

✈ Do what you can.

Dear Parent,

At kids POWer hour we learned that we must use our hands to help ourselves and others.

✓ Try it. Help your child color and cut out this Handy Kid label. If you have rubber cement, coat the back and let dry to make a sticker.

Let your child wear this sticker as he does a special job for you. (Attach with a safety pin if you do not have rubber cement.)

Let your child hear you tell others often what "a handy kid" he is. Praise motivates a child to work like nothing else.

✓ Pray about it. Pray with your child asking God to show you ways you can help others. Thank God for healthy hands and bodies that can work.

kids
POWer
hour
staff

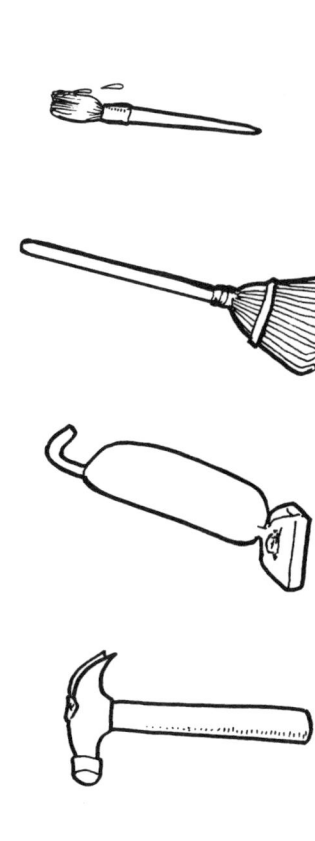

take home paper ages 7-11

At God's House

Name _____

Powerhouse 12

Do you remember the difference in the brothers, "Slothful and Sluggard" and "Diligence and Zeal"?
✏ Write the words from the word bank under the pictures of the brothers which the words describe.

| Slothful | Sluggard | Diligence | Zeal |

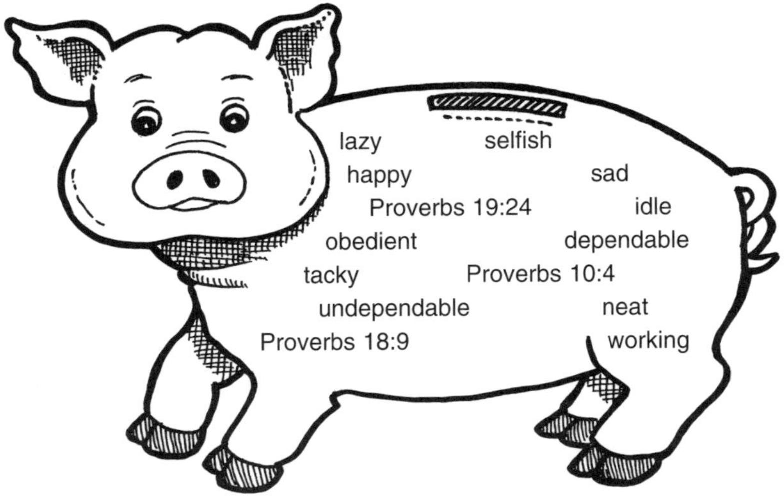

Word bank (on pig):
lazy, happy, selfish, sad, Proverbs 19:24, idle, dependable, obedient, tacky, Proverbs 10:4, undependable, neat, Proverbs 18:9, working

✏ Lay your hand on this paper and trace around it. On each finger and the thumb write one thing your working hands can do to help someone else.

Do what you can.

Thank God for two strong, healthy hands.

At Your House

Permission to photocopy this page granted for church use.

At Your House

13

✝ **Praise God whatever the circumstances.**

Dear Parent,

Sometimes we do not feel like praising the Lord, but we learned at kids POWer hour that that is the time we need to. Paul and Silas praised God in prison, and God delivered them.

Here are some suggestions of things you can do to help your child become aware of times when "bragging on Jesus" will get His attention.

✓ Play it. Do a role play. Pretend you are sick and show how you could praise the Lord. Let your child pretend he has a broken arm. Use a scarf for a sling. Give him several small tasks to do. Encourage him to praise the Lord even when he is having trouble doing simple jobs. Explain that if the situation had been real, you would praise the Lord, and your child should, too.

✓ Pray with your child. Start your prayer time with praise. Emphasize that first we got God's attention. Then we make our requests. End your prayer with praise. Point out to your child that praise is like the bread on a sandwich. Prayer starts and ends with praise.

kids POWer hour staff

At God's House

We should brag on Jesus even in trouble. Trace Paul and Silas' words. Color and cut out the picture. Stand it in your room as a reminder to praise the Lord even when you do not feel like it.

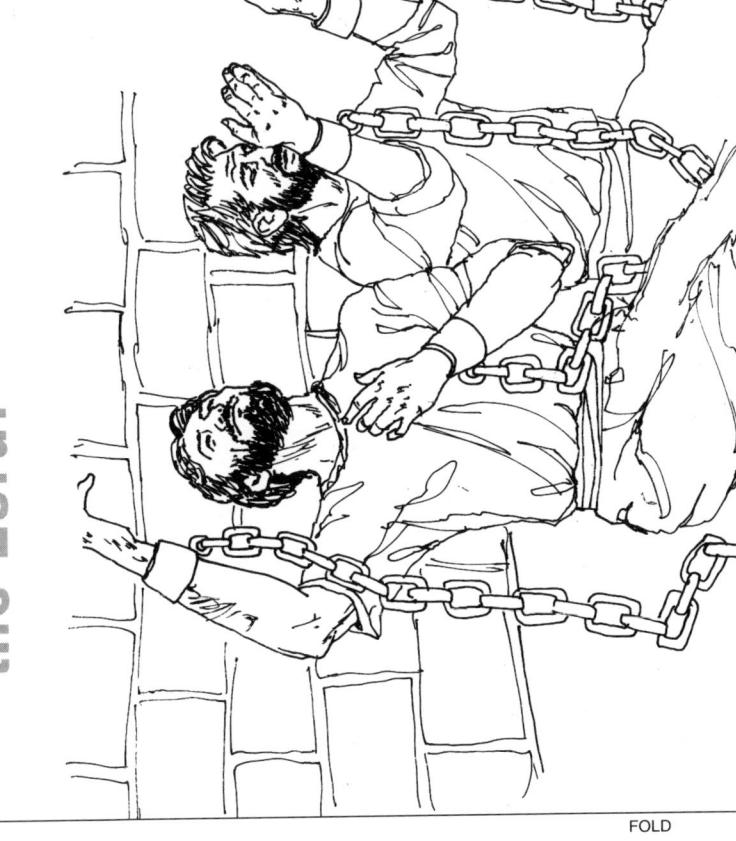

Praise the Lord! Hallelujah!

take home paper ages 4-6

Permission to photocopy this page granted for church use.

take home paper ages 7-11

Powerhouse 1B

At God's House

Paul and Silas praised God even while suffering in prison. Probably we will never be thrown into a dark, cold, damp prison, but we will certainly face trying circumstances. That's when we need to brag on Jesus. We get His attention when we praise Him.

✏️ Around this circle are some circumstances which come to us in life. Write the capital letters on the line below to know how to be joyful no matter what the circumstances. Start with the capital "P."

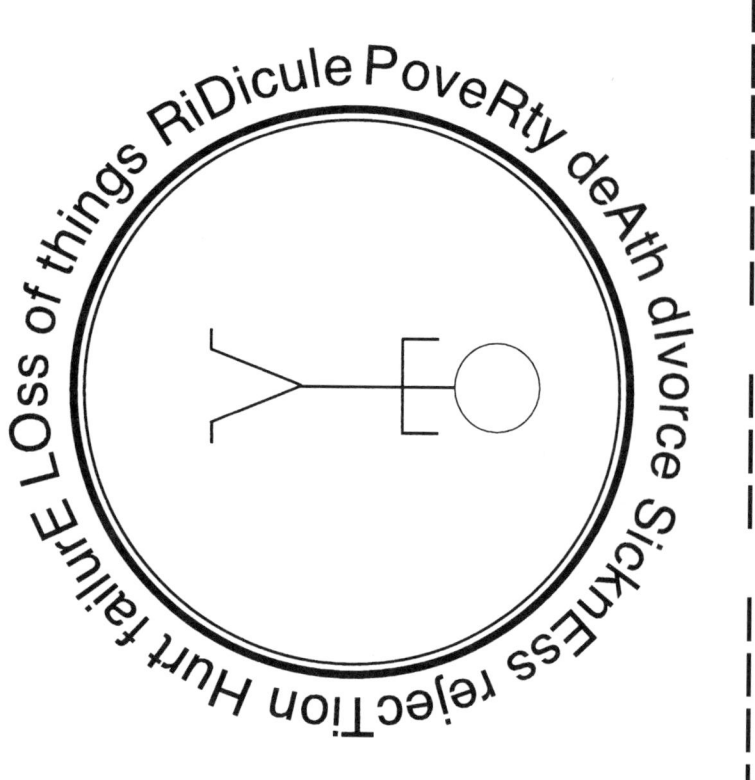

___ ___ ___ ___ ___ ___ ___ ___ ___ ___ ___ ___ ___ ___ ___ ___

things RiDicule PoveRty deAth dIvorce Sickness rejecTion Hurt failurE LOSs of

At Your House

 **Praise God whatever the circumstances.**

At home make a personal "Praise Book." Place several sheets of typing paper on a sheet of construction paper. Fold in the middle and staple or fasten together with yarn. Find verses in the Book of Psalms which say, "Praise the Lord." Copy these into your "Praise Book." Decorate the cover (construction paper). When you are in unpleasant circumstances, read these Psalms aloud.

Construction paper

Fold and staple or tie with yarn

several sheets white paper

Decorate cover

Permission to photocopy this page granted for church use.

Permission granted to copy art for local church use.

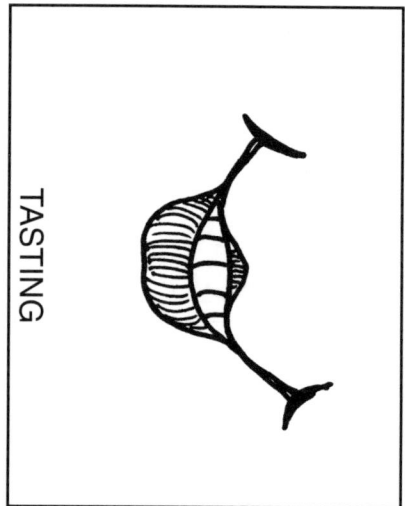
TASTING

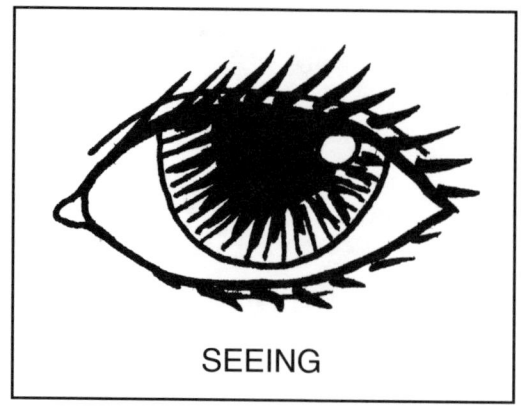
SEEING

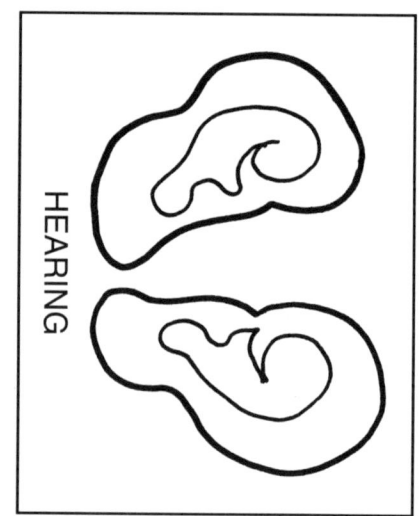
HEARING

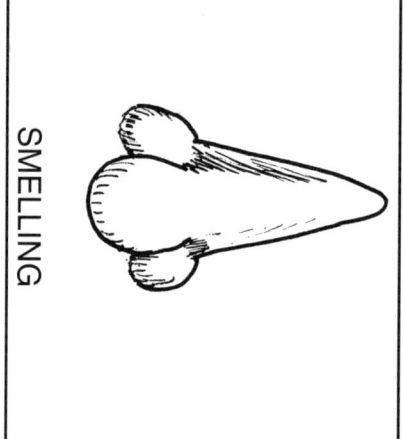
SMELLING

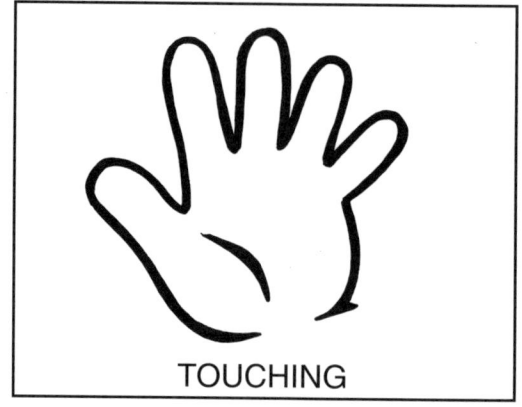
TOUCHING

Permission granted to copy art for local church use.

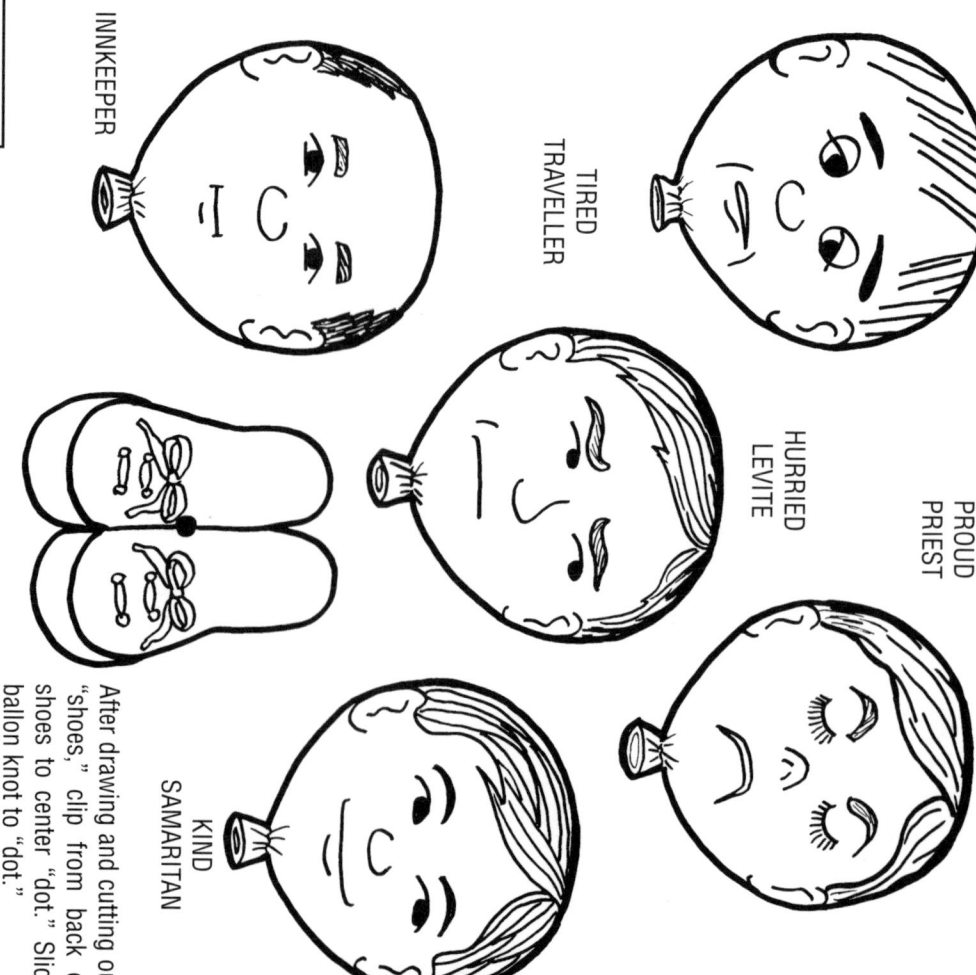

INNKEEPER

TIRED TRAVELLER

HURRIED LEVITE

PROUD PRIEST

KIND SAMARITAN

After drawing and cutting out "shoes," clip from back of shoes to center "dot." Slide balloon knot to "dot."

Permission granted to copy art for local church use.

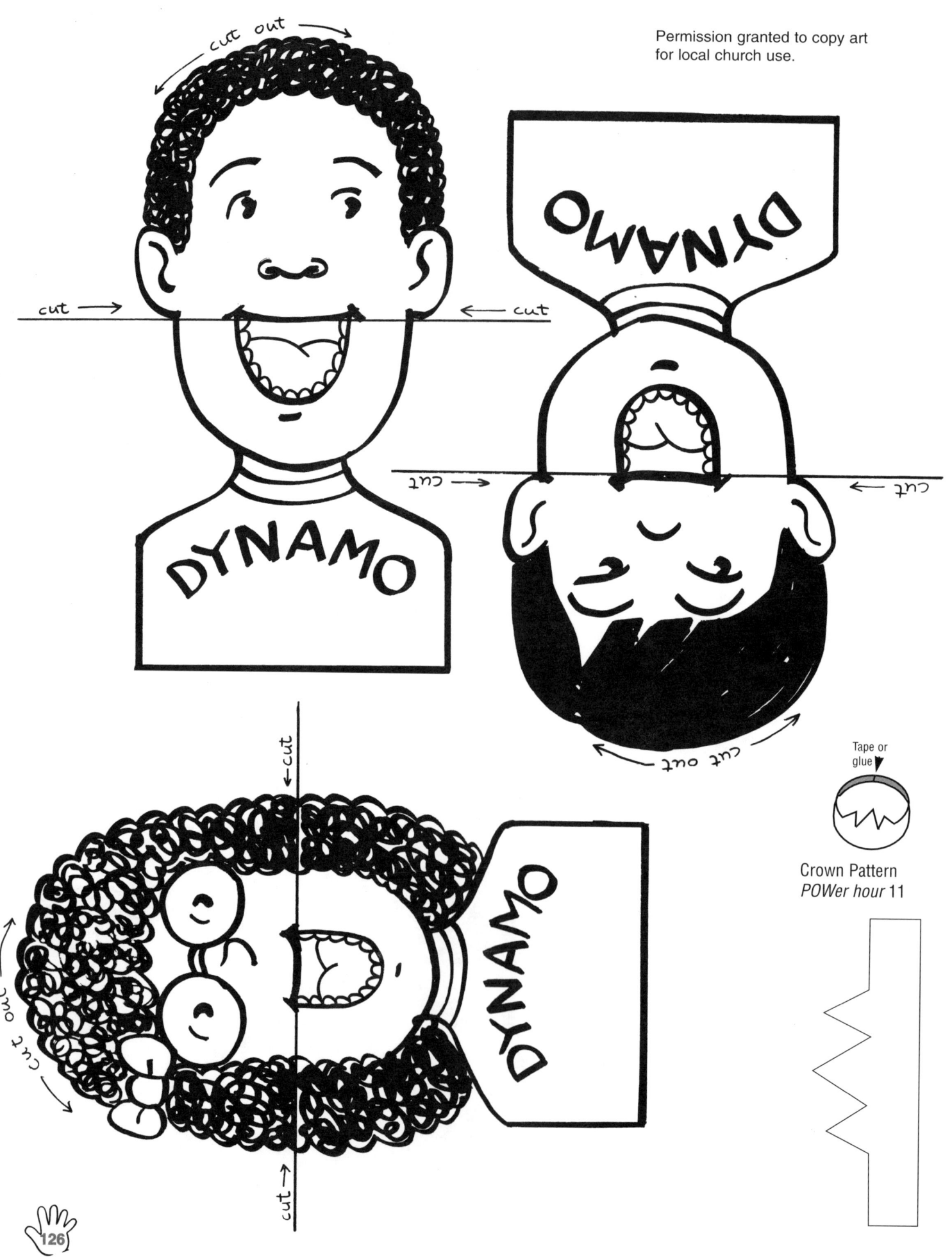

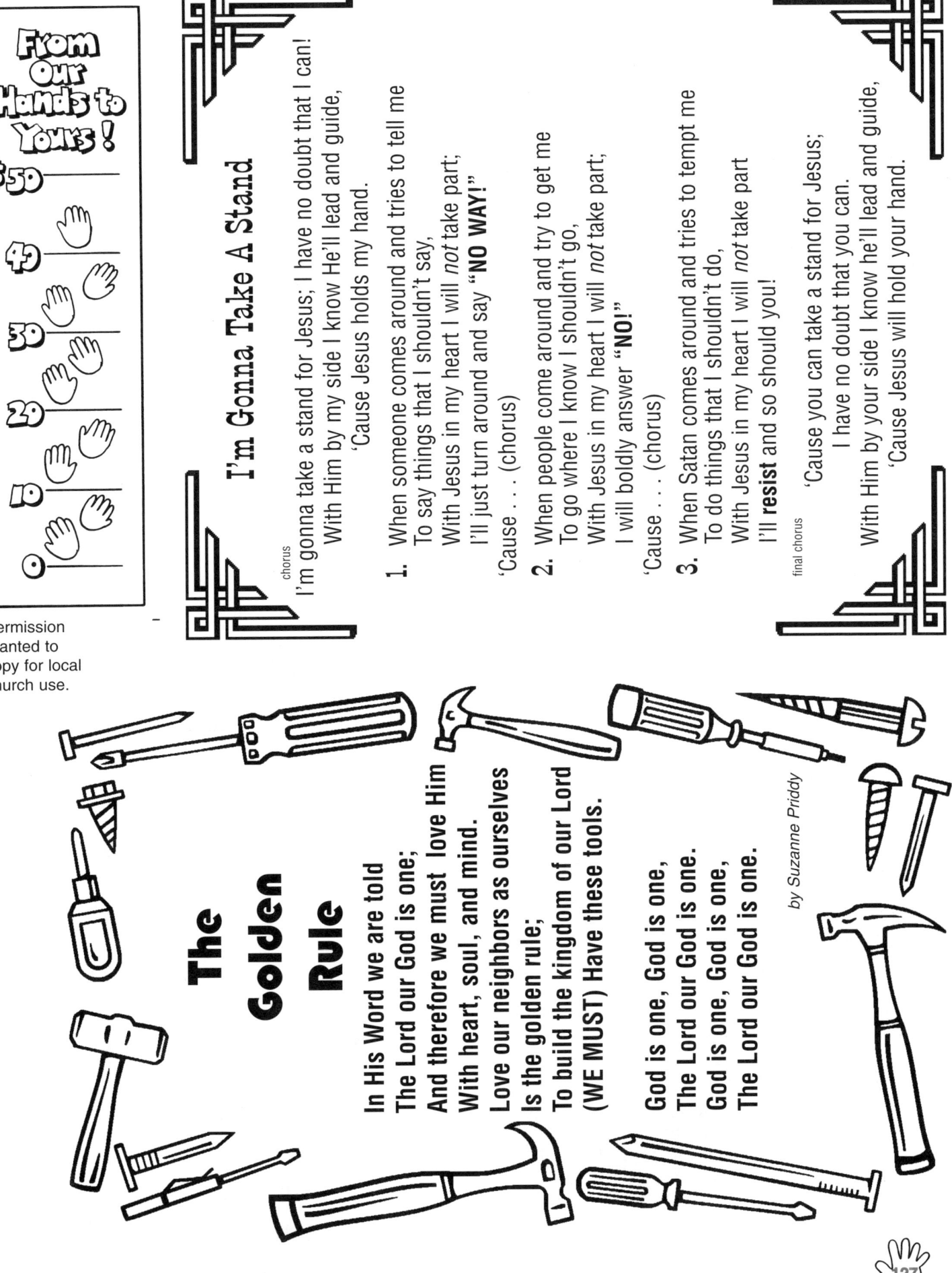

Puppet Stage

HELPFUL TIP:
Rev. Ron Rice of Calvary Evangelism Center, Sacramento, CA, suggested using felt for the curtains. With an overhead projector, enlarge art to make felt background scenes, and use flannelgraph style.

Stage is constructed of 1" PVC pipe. Six 1" ells and eight 1" tees are required. Six 10' sections of 1" PVC are required.

NOTE: To make stage a permanent construction, glue all joints. To make stage portable, glue indicated joints on both sides of stage.

6 inches
1 inch TEE
1 inch ELL
5 feet
3 inches
3 inches
4 feet 6 inches
5 feet
7 feet
NO GLUE
GLUE
GLUE
NO GLUE
NO GLUE
NO GLUE
GLUE
GLUE
GLUE